A 2nd Anthology of Radical Thoughts & Empowering Perspectives

Dr. Marcus M. Mottley

First Edition
Library of Congress Cataloging-in-Publication Data

ISBN: 1542997178
ISBN-13: 9781542997171

Dedication

*For the sons and daughters of Antigua and Barbuda!
Be ever watchful! Get up - rise up and rid our country of
the corrupt leaders and want-to-be leaders who have no
qualms about selling our children's birthrights, selling all
of our assets, selling our future... so that they can grab
the proceeds for them and theirs!*

Table of Contents

Acknowledgements

I **ACKNOWLEDGE AND** thank the Antiguan and Barbudan warriors who fight every day to protect our country from both local and foreign marauders. I thank those who speak, those who write, those who bring a public candle to the hidden deals made by the corrupt and the corruptible. I thank those who in any way – quietly, secretly, publicly, privately or prayerfully agitate to protect the progeny of generations of Antiguan and Barbudan Slaves from the modern day piratical moves and maneuvers of foreign financiers and also from the machinations of the so-called 'local' marauding business class.

Section 1

Radical Thoughts

What Place Is This? Who Are We?

January, 1990

What place is this?
Where lands are sold
    To politicians and their cronies
    For farthings and pennies
And then resold
    Not for shillings...
    But for gold

What place is this?
Where lands are sold
    To hungry white trash
    A pack of wolves who without a fight
    Will grab everything with their cash
    And now they control our soil, our lands
    With money grabbing hands... that soil my birthright.

What place is this?
Where Lebanese and Syrians
    Or whatever they be
Who mercenaries and ruffians

Ran from their home country.
Now they own everything that by right
   Really belongs to me.

What place is this?
Where one man – a foreigner –
   An albino
Owns and controls all the energy:
   Gas, petrol, diesel –
   and even holds a lien on the electricity.
All a-we paying he – All a ah-we hard earned money
   And he – getting all a that tax free;
You know that some flying politicians get them dunny
   Yep.... big, big money kickback from he!

What place is this?
Where the Government gets a little tax and duty,
   And the politicians collect the big pay-offs
   For giving away licenses free
   And making personal deals with the people's property?

What place is this?
Where Cable & Wireless have a monopoly...
   A strangle hold on all communications in the country
Where ah-we-the people collect some small tax
   And the British C & W
   Carry away all the dunny plus the gravy?

What place is this?
Where we don't control our gas
   and the power source of energy
Where we don't own shares
   in the lucrative communications industry?
Where our lands, resources and documents

Are given away like sweetie by a fat *cutie*
So that he can illegally make all foreigners happy?

What manner of people are we?
   Afraid to speak openly...
   Muzzled into shame and guilty soliloquy
   Unable to think independently?
   Settling for some pittance and tiny salary...
   While politicians and their albino friends
   Line their coffers with stolen birthrights – ah we only property?

What manner of people are we
   That we refuse to wrench power from those
   Who are corrupt and practice grand thievery?
   Who sink to the lowest depths
   so that they can enrich themselves with our money...
   Scavengers, skunks, vultures – preying on our island society...

When will the people rise up?
It is time 'nuff now for them to stop!
   Let's give them their due...
Let them feel the anger, the vengeance
   the strong feelings long pent up...
Let all ah dem feel the frustration of a nation
   Betrayed by our own...
   Some ah them once beloved
And lets do away that that obscene family monopoly

Who are we?
We are a people – who will no longer suffer silently
We will make the hard change...
And we will do it...
   By any means necessary!

From Slavery to Servitude to Service

March, 1990

Servitude
    Slavery –
        Bondage
        Work without pay

Servitude
    Domination
        Owned by another
            Live in misery

Servitude
    White over black
        For their instant gain
            Our continuous pain

Servitude
    17th, 18th & 19th Century
        Sad days in World History
            But that's still our story

Servitude
    Sugar cane and cotton
        We plough the fields
            Oh Lord, memories of chigger & dysentery
            Oh me belly...
            Me belly hut me.

Servitude
    Plantations
        Masters & slaves
            Domination by rape and murder
            A game? No... that's our reality...
                Our not so distant history

Service
    Plantations
        We grow the cane... we cut the cane
        We make the sugar
        They ship it and sell it in the North lands
        They keep all the sweet money
            Up there in them country

Service
    Tourism
        Our #1 so-called industry
            Have we gone crazy?
            Turning our back on the past?
                Insanity!

Service
    Serve their meals
    Make their beds
    Smile so you get their money
    Strategies of the great widdy widdy grand daddy?

Service
    Be nice
    Watch your attitude!
    Smile and keep your chin up!
    We don't want them to go to Europe!

Service
    Servitude
        White over Black
        They own the hotels
        Of course they keep the big money
            In them far off country

Service
    Plantation
        They own the beach front property
        We clean the house and the yard
            for little more than a penny...
        And they keeping all the sweet money
            In them far off country

Service
    Domination
        By foreign banks
            Lend us the money
            Them own ah we
            No way out of this financial slavery

Tourism
    Servitude
    Domination
    Foreign ownership
        At them whim and mercy

White over Black
    17th, 18th & 19th Century?
No! 20th & 21st Century

Slavery, Servitude, Service
    And, still
    Sad days in our history
    Still... Lord have mercy.
Massah no wan free me...
    And still,
        Me 'fraid for fight he!

Slavery, Servitude, Service
    He still ha me a serve he
    And he still control from far away in fuh he country
    Them still a tell me for smiley smiley
    But me tired ah this burden and cruelty
    Oh Lord help me...
        Please help ah-we!

Headlines

May, 1990

U.S. opposes NATO strategy shift
U.S. should be the first to fire Nuclear weapons in a war
U.S. must gain military superiority
U.S. ready to debate the end of chemical arms production
U.S. opposes Third World program while Europe supports the plan
    for chlorofluorocarbon reduction
Jews deliver warning at the site of "Final Solution"
Jews afraid of a United Germany because it reminds them of
    holocaust and tyranny

Regulators to U.S. Banks: "Keep lending!"
Even though economic statistics show troubles in the market
    increasing
GOP candidates sent reeling by Bush decision to open door to
    tax increases
Lesbian Union sanctioned by Methodist denomination
    giving their blessing to same sex unions
While Barney Frank again denies involvement in a ring of
    prostitution.

Senate study triples cocaine users estimate so Biden calls
    for new spending

Bennet claims figures are pure politicking.
Meanwhile Marion Barry awaits political fate
While prosecutors keep adding more charges while still probing.
Panamanians seek damage for U.S. invasion which reportedly
     killed and maimed thousands of innocent civilians.

U.S. seeks wider anti-drug powers
     and 'aliens' could face summary expulsion.
Van Gogh painting gets $82.5 million dollars
     Portrait of Dr. Gachet taken by Japanese buyer.
Bush to sign Civil Rights Bill supposedly restoring rights
     eroded by Supreme Court decision.
And Sununu says that Bush will employ the axe
     if Democrats propose any type of tax.

U.S. blame Sandanistas for Violeta Chamorros troubles
     While workers there strike for wage increases.
Chamorros says "My country is bankrupt"
     She doesn't say it's due to Americas trade blockade!
Bush conspires to see White South African leader
     just before the historic visit of Nelson Mandela.
Two U.S. soldiers killed in Manila
     And, Philippines resent American destruction of their culture.
U.S. urged to keep forces in NATO
     to give American superiority and advantage in the future.
Governor Wilder orders Virginia divestment policy regarding South
     Africa
     thereby making this governor the conscience of America!

Fiscal Imbalance

April 2003

Fiscal imbalance or fiscal incompetence?
Fiscal imbalance or publicly insolvent?
Fiscal imbalance or criminal fraudulence?
Fiscal imbalance or downright poor governance?

The airport...
Given to the new Moody Stuart massa...
While Air traffic controllers
Have no water... no elevator... Not even radar...
Putting everyone's life potentially in danger.
Airport functions in jeopardy – its facilities so shabby
That its international standing – now the laughing stock of the industry
And, remember the $11Million brother
Now the prime one has got his many pieces of silver...
Talking about the #1 minister...
Spoils collected from the foreigner turned-so-called citizen-investor...
Who doles out bribes for favors – this new colonial land & property grabber!

Fiscal imbalance or fiscal incompetence?
Fiscal imbalance or publicly insolvent?

Fiscal imbalance or criminal fraudulence?
Fiscal imbalance or downright poor governance?

The hospital
Over-budget... money in someone's pocket?
They all lined up to feast...
Including some from the Far East and the two from City East...
Yes... also talking about that turncoat candidate...
And we'll still be at the mercy of Dr. Dead...
And we'll pay dearly for his experiments on our heart and head...
All of this while planning to push out local nurses
Scheming to continue lining their already full purses...
Look again... see the long arm of the new Moody Stuart...
Leeching all aspects of our fragile economic climate...
And leaving us in the industry dirt and permanently fiscally hurt

Fiscal imbalance or fiscal incompetence?
Fiscal imbalance or publicly insolvent?
Fiscal imbalance or criminal fraudulence?
Fiscal imbalance or downright poor governance?

Government worker
In the words of the #1 Minister – the Baby Vulture...
You get your salary... "better late than never"
"You have a job... continue to be thankful to Papa"
"We hire you...even though ah you no work"
Teacher, ex-hospital administrator, nurse or clerk
"Ah you ungrateful to this good red shirt gang party..."
You must work without pay... an' give to you country...
Vote us back in and you will get your money – maybe...

Fiscal imbalance or fiscal incompetence?
Fiscal imbalance or publicly insolvent?

Fiscal imbalance or criminal fraudulence?
Fiscal imbalance or downright poor governance?

The country...
Electricity – off every day...
While people still charged the same money...
Water – off every day – from June to May...
While the saltwater plant sends water back to the sea...
Schools without books, supplies, desks & basic equipment
Students suffer from the woefully deprived environment...
Agricultural lands... acres given to agents and friends
Such as the new Moody Stuart – he getting ebryting...
Government buildings – leaky and falling apart...
The Syrians and others – with big property 'deed and contract...
That Vulture Family of the #1 Minister – "dem no hab no heart!"

Fiscal imbalance or fiscal incompetence?
Fiscal imbalance or publicly insolvent?
Fiscal imbalance or criminal fraudulence?
Fiscal imbalance or downright poor governance?

The economy
Good, positive growth is the claim
It's so good that teachers can't be paid...
    Met Officers – the same
    Air Traffic Controllers – the same
    Public Work employees – the same...
What a shame....
That even those at the Treasury...
Took action to expose the scandalous numbers game
The economic plan: Borrow bank money to pay salary
And use public lands as loan surety...
No evidence of economic growth
Plenty evidence of economic sloth....

Fiscal imbalance? No!
Incompetence!
Criminal fraudulence!
Politically bankrupt and insolvent!
And, downright poor governance!

The leadership
Baby Vulture and he government propped up by foreign massas
Who entice ministers and key representatives with ill-gotten dollars
All 'a dem' guilty of receiving bribes and illegal tithes
So that the new Moody Stuart massa can tief ah we birth rights
Even the banks' decision to rescue the bankrupt regime
Is ill conceived – and may sink us deeper downstream
Be careful of breathing new life into this cancer...
It won't take much for them to metastasize –
Then win another election and hasten the national demise..
Yes, they might survive and get a reprise ...
By throwing around money given by the real leader...
Not Baby Vulture... but the foreign investor –
What does that Stand for? – He is the Moody Stuart massa –
The cowboy de facto governor of Antigua-Barbuda!

Fiscal imbalance? No!
Ineptitude and dishonesty!
Corruption and bribery – all a dem guilty!
Unconscionable behavior by the Red Shirt Party!
Criminal malpractice & certified insanity!

Questions About Antigua

November, 2003

WHAT ECONOMIC PROGRAMS will save Antigua and Barbuda? Can we get beyond our one eyed, polyphemic posture... that keeps us locked to tourism... Can we not look to agri-industries, fisheries, software development, data entry and data processing services, micro manufacturing industries, internet business services, international banking and financial services,

And if we stick to tourism, how can we take it to another level? How can we develop a unique tourist product – one that is different from every other island in the Caribbean? Do we have people with the vision and the courage and audacity to challenge the Bahamas, etc.?

How is education in schools linked to our economic future? What strategic plans have been developed to prepare our children for a life beyond tourism... to prepare our children to be more than waiters and waitresses? Where are the new teacher education programs – to prepare them for teaching in the 21st Century? Where are the new classrooms to prepare our students to compete in the 21st Century? Where is the training in Administrative and organizational leadership for our school principals so that they can manage and run our schools efficiently and lead their staff professionally? Where are the programs that link schools to business to properly prepare our students to work in private sector organizations? Where are the continuing education programs for our nurses so that they can master the new technological instruments and machines used in modern medicine? Where are the continuing education programs for our technical and professional workers – from APUA to the Met Office, from the Control tower to Public Works, from the Police to the Defense force, from ABS TV to Public Health Officers?

What plans have been developed to stimulate the development of entrepreneurial activity in Antigua and Barbuda? What plans have been crafted to kindle and promote and support the aspiring young business start-ups in our twin island state? What monies have been identified and set aside... what resources have been allocated... what services have been created to help our entrepreneurs turn their ideas into successful small businesses and their small businesses into the large conglomerates?

Are our leaders saying that we can't do any of these? That we have to depend on foreign dirty money which needs to be laundered through our economy? Are our leaders saying that our people – don't have what it takes to build our own country? That we need to invite foreigners from distant shores to lord it over us?

What new and exciting ideas do our leaders... those who have been at the helm for 27+ years and those that want to be our new leaders... have for the future of Antigua?

What is their vision? What challenging goals do they have that go beyond the normal – build another hotel, build a bigger hotel, build a fancier hotel, etc? What vision do they have that go beyond begging money, receiving bribes, selling our land for personal favors, not only mortgaging our birthrights but the birthrights of our children? What vision do they have that go beyond trying to entice new Moody Stuarts, new colonialists – egotistical investors who see the Caribbean as their new frontier, who see the people of the Caribbean like how Pizarro and Cortez and Columbus saw the Incas, the Aztecs and the Arawaks?

What is the real agenda of these new colonialists – these pirates – whether from Texas or Colombia... whether they are Jewish or English...? Can we not use history as our lesson?

Are we satisfied... with the notion that so and so pirate investor is our saviour? And, therefore, because they pay well, they bring a lot of jobs... that they are good for our country? And because of all that... that we should give them our lands... give them our pristine islands, give them our best real estate...? Are we satisfied with the notion that these new Moody Stuarts, Henry Morgans and Black Beards are our only hope? And if we are satisfied, what has brought us to this? Is this healthy?

And why Antigua? Why, did they not go elsewhere? Do you think they could do this in Jamaica? Guyana? Trinidad? Barbados? Even St. Kitts? And if not, why not? What is it about Antigua (I can't say Barbuda – at least not yet) – What is it about us... our leaders – that makes us attractive to them? What about us makes us vulnerable to their vulgar and obscene overtures... what makes our politicians say yes and submit to their indecent proposals and corrupting overtures? What allows our leaders to prostitute our country to the most offensive offers and accept the most crude behaviors from these Pirates of the Caribbean?

Unethical Behavior in Public Office:

An American and Antiguan & Barbudan Dilemma?

February 2006

AMERICA'S TOP POLITICAL leaders in Washington are ducking for cover! This unusual situation was recently triggered when multi-millionaire and well connected lobbyist Jack Abramoff pleaded guilty to federal charges of conspiracy, tax evasion and mail fraud. Among other things, Abramoff was charged in a conspiracy involving "corruption of public officials" by providing campaign contributions, expensive gifts, trips and other items in exchange for certain "official acts." As part of his plea and a deal he is making with the government, Abramoff has agreed to tell federal prosecutors about huge donations and lavish gifts he gave members of Congress in exchange for their support and influence.

As a result, Federal prosecutors are currently investigating more than twenty-five lawmakers and staff members in connection with Abramoff and his wheeling and dealing.

"We need to reform the rules so it's clear beyond a shadow of a doubt what is ethically acceptable for members of Congress, of the House of Representatives and their staff," Hastert, an Illinois Republican, told reporters. The problem with Hastert's statement is that under his leadership and the leadership of Frist in the Senate, for years they have aggressively resisted bi-partisan efforts to buttress the rules governing the behaviors of the members of Congress.

Additionally, Hastert and his Republican colleagues thumbed their noses at public calls for an independent investigation of Tom DeLay, the Republican Congressional Majority Leader. As a matter of fact, one of their first tasks in on January 4th 2005, was to pass a rule which made it difficult for Congress to investigate its own members. Now, exactly one year later, the tables have been flipped.

What about Antigua & Barbuda?
So what does this American political soap opera have to do with Antigua & Barbuda? The answers ought to be clear if we review over twenty five years of hundreds of charges of corruption laid at the feet of the former administration and the resulting culture of corruption that their misbehavior fostered among public officials generally and elected officials in particular. The relationship to what's happening in America is also relevant when we look at the less than two years of the current administration and the charges that have been laid at the feet of a few officials of the new Government.

It is true that the new Government swept into office promising transparency and accountability. It is also true that, unlike Hastert and Frist, the Baldwin Spencer Administration moved quickly to deal with conflict of interest charges against two government officials involved in questions over the Digicel matter. Unlike Hastert and Frist, Prime Minister Spencer similarly quickly responded to requests for an independent investigation into the APUA matter.

The Prime Minister and his Administration should pay close attention to the critical issues that gave rise to the current ethical upheaval in Washington. The key issue that contributed to what's happening now is that Jack Abramoff was being investigated and has struck a deal with Federal prosecutors. In other words, even though he had the ear of powerful friends in the legislative body, another part of the government, the judiciary, investigated him and charged him! And, as a result, the government (judiciary) is investigating, and will probably bring corruption charges against members of the legislature.

In Antigua & Barbuda, we need to demonstrate that we have the legal structure, legal authority and judicial will to allow our judiciary do its job, without pressure or influence from the legislative and executive bodies.

Yes, we have the laws (Integrity in Public Office) that protect us from the corruptive behaviors of public officials (legislature and executive). Yes, we have the Code of Conduct enshrined in that legal framework. And yes, we have, I think, a Code which governs the principled conduct of public officials *and* civil servants.

However, what we need most is the trust and confidence that all of these mechanisms will be applied freely and independently of political interference and influence. This is the principal issue that we in Antigua and Barbuda must put in place.

Influence Peddling

There is one other issue that I am duty bound to highlight. Jack Abramoff was a freewheeling and free-spending influence-monger who used his contacts and his money to sway politicians and influence governmental decisions.

What can Antiguans and Barbudans learn from this?
We must be ever vigilant when dealing with the influence peddlers among us. We know who they are. They have used their financial power to influence politicians in the past. They have bought the allegiance of politicians in the past. They have greased the palms of government officers (high and low) in the past. They have used their money to play both sides of the fence... for their financial and property gains.

They have not changed. They 'may' still be doing these things. Some may have found 'community' ways to influence leaders... both here and throughout the Caribbean. Their gifts, just like Jack

Abramoff's gifts, come with, at the very least, an expectancy of advantageous favors, positions and in some cases 'rights'.

And there is one other thing. Some of these Abramoff' type influence peddling "Pirates in the Caribbean" have also wheeled and 'dealed' with members of the American Congress. From past experience we know that they have certainly wheeled, 'dealed' and dined here with Antiguan and Barbudan politicians and public officials. The Baldwin Spencer Administration needs to move cautiously when working with these high flying influence peddlers.

One only has to listen to the concerns of Antiguans as they call in to their favorite radio shows to know that there is deep public concern about past corruption among public officials and the fact that things may not have changed all that much with the new Administration.

There can be no question that at least one thing has changed. Baldwin Spencer and his administration have put the legislation in place that can be used to target public corruption and unethical behavior among public officials. Now they must demonstrate the will to use that legislation with every opportunity they get – no matter who the violator is.

I am convinced at this time that Mr. Spencer is fully committed to the highest standards of principled leadership. I have no doubt that he will lead in ways that boost the public's trust and confidence, and demonstrate that he and his Cabinet Ministers are serious about their dual promises of transparency *and* accountability not only in their public activities but also in their private endeavors.

Writing On The Wall

February, 2006

I HAVE TAKEN it upon myself to read, re-read and read again the writings of one of Antigua's giants of history, economy and philosophy: Tim Hector.

As much as I have been dumfounded by the political company he kept in his later years, this pales in comparison to the awe in which I hold the man for his insight, clarity in articulation and depth of perspective that he exhibited in is earlier years.

And so, I would like to share with you a few paragraphs from a 1996 "Fan the Flame" Article entitled: "Lester Bird Broke the Neck of the Economy".

> *"It is not an accident that the 'best and brightest' in Antigua over the last twenty years did not go into the productive and creative sectors. They went into traditional professions, law, medicine, teaching. Few went into management, engineering, marketing. This was because the productive sectors of the Antigua and Barbuda economy became even more underdeveloped between 1976-1996.*
>
> *We are going to suffer in the future from this lack of trained personnel for modern industrial and productive*

activity. Besides, the free movement of skilled labour in all CARICOM territories, is going to make Antigua & Barbuda a net importer of skilled labour. This together with the fact, that nearly one-third of the Antigua labour force some 7,300 workers are already 'foreign nationals' will complicate both politics and economics here. The economy is a thorough-going Bird mess."

Imagine that Tim Hector in 1996 was predicting that we would suffer from the "lack of trained personnel for modern industrial and productive activity." Listen to the nurses at Holberton, have a discussion with a police officer, call your child's teacher, talk with your mechanic... the chances are that you would be speaking with someone from either Cuba, Guyana, Jamaica, St. Vincent... and well... even Dominica! And if you speak with a business owner in English Harbour, Redcliffe Key or a real estate agent from addresses unknown – you will be speaking with someone from Wisconsin, Texas, Singapore, Germany, Canada, Syria, Lebanon, China or some such place!

Furthermore, Tim Hector saw what would happen with the advent of CSME! "The free movement of skilled labor... will make Antigua and Barbuda a net importer of skilled labour." All because our political leaders failed to influence, encourage, motivate and stimulate young Antiguans and Barbudans to go into the 'productive and creative' sectors! And, it is my contention that the threat from Caribbean nationals pales in comparison to the future hegemonic threat from the neo-colonialists (economic pirates and privateers) from North America and Europe. (But that is another discussion for another article.)

Tim Hector continues: *"Simultaneously, Antigua and Barbuda, under successive Bird administrations did nothing to develop its human resources: from management through entry level labourers. That is, did nothing to train managers and provide labourers with skills. There was no plan. Therefore, those things dignified with the name "skills training"*

*were pork-barrel patronage programmes, to provide workers to exist-
ing firms, with the government paying millions of dollars which went
down the drain. These millions added to the disastrous assembly type
foray, made awful financial matters worse. No project instituted under
the aegis of Lester Bird has ever worked. Each and every one has always
been a drain on the national treasury."*

Not only did millions of dollars go down the drain... so did the
talents and aspirations of thousands of children in primary and secondary schools. They looked around and they saw few opportunities for a robust economic future. They looked around and saw their
mothers and fathers, uncles and aunts going to dead end jobs, learn-
ing nothing new and doing nothing creative, sitting at desks twid-
dling their thumbs, passing ledgers from one desk to another: under
productive – underperforming – underemployed!

These same children had a window to the world through CNN,
MTV, Cartoon Network and Nickelodeon. They kind of knew that it
was different elsewhere... that there was a mismatch between what
was happening in Antigua and Barbuda... and the rest of the world.

These children watched as they moved from Infant 1 to Junior 5...
and noticed that their teachers were changing... that the doctors in the
clinics were changing... that the nurses at the hospital were changing...

These children watched as successive governments were unable
or unwilling to find an Antiguan or Barbudan who could serve as
Attorney General. When they went to the National Museum, they
found a non-Antiguan/Barbudan telling them about our history.

All around them, their uncles, aunts, and cousins had been mar-
ginalized and in some ways made irrelevant to the national scheme
of things. And somewhere in the inner consciousness they knew that
their future chances were limited... their birthrights are being stolen
right from under them... their futures are dim... and they know it.
Go to any school... Ottos, Bendals, Golden Grove, Pigotts... look into
their eyes... I can tell you... these are not the eyes that I saw when I
taught in 1978. No.

I am from Perry Bay... Tinning Village... Grays Farm. Born and bred. I taught at Greenbay School. Each time I pass through the area... I see the children of students that I taught... hanging on the corners. I even see their parents hanging on the other side of those same corners. Unemployed. Underemployed. And some... well... unaccustomed to employment.

And, each time I pass... or walk by... someone looks up through eyes dimmed with pain and disillusionment and shouts, "Mr. Mottley!" Or, "Teacher!" And, tears come to my heart and find a path to my eyes.

Anyone who dismisses the more than quarter century of "Birdonomics" as just another set of chapters in our history, have not really walked through Grays Farm, Point, Bendals or Old Road with their eyes open. They, like some of my former students, have been numbed and drugged by years of abandonment by the political elite, or by the fact they were blinded by their own marginal successes.

Tim Hector in his 1996 article, called for the then Bird government to change the way they did business. As pre-requisites to any success, he called for *"an accountable government, free of scandal, which can mobilise the public for the economic tasks at hand. Nothing else will do. The more we wait, the worse it will become. Time is against us. A scandal-ridden regime, **cannot**, repeat, cannot, mobilise any nation, anywhere, anytime. Need I say more? The economic writing is on the wall, for all to see and read. Those who will not hear, the old adage goes, will feel. Nothing educates like feeling."*

"The economic writing is on the wall." Today, February 17th, 2006, fully ten years after Hector wrote his article, we have a new administration. Yet, it is not clear to me that we have been fully educated by the failures of the past. My heart is still crying not only for the plight of my former students, but for the condition that their children and grandchildren find themselves in. I am yet to see any changes in Greenbay, Grays Farm, Point, Bendals or Old Road. I am yet to feel any sense of hopefulness and motivation.

I see even more foreign nurses, teachers, mechanics and police officers – not to mention accountants, lawyers, attorneys general... even portfolio-less, foreign born, appointed ministers of government!

I am yet to see a major initiative to address the plight of indigenous Antiguans and Barbudans, to increase their skill levels, enhance their professional training and qualifications so that they can raise themselves out of the quagmire (mud) in which they were abandoned by the former and, now, seemingly ignored by the current.

We cannot wait for the economy to be right. We cannot wait for the deficit to be reduced. We cannot wait for the programmes to move from the drawing board. We have waited for over a quarter century.

"The economic writing is on the wall." The social writing is in our face. We need real change, real **fast!**

Blood Diamonds & Blood Money

October 2006

IN JANUARY 2006, the film Blood Diamonds was nominated for five Academy Awards including Best Actor (Leonardo DiCaprio) and Best Supporting Actor (Djimon Hounsou). Set in the Sierra Leone Civil War, the film portrays a country torn apart by a struggle between sides equally vicious and heedless of the suffering of innocent non-combatants.

Blood diamonds are gems that have been used by rebel groups to fund armed conflict and civil war. This film draws attention to the devastating impact the trade in blood diamonds has had in countries such as Sierra Leone, Angola and the Democratic Republic of Congo, where billions of dollars of profits from the sale of diamonds have been used to fuel brutal wars.

Diamonds mined in the rebel-held north of Ivory Coast, in West Africa, are currently reaching the international diamond market, and there are credible reports of massive diamond smuggling from Zimbabwe into South Africa and Belgium in violation of an international ban on these 'blood diamonds.'

Thus far, much of the focus on who benefits from this has been spotlighted on the various African rebel groups and their blood thirsty leaders. Maybe 'money and power thirsty' might be a better characterization of them. However, what's missing in descriptions of the blood diamond trade is that not only are companies like the

South African diamond giant De Beers being charged with obscenely profiting from the illegal trade, but diamond sellers in every city in Europe and America have blood on their hands also.

In addition, there is a new documentary, "Blood on a Stone" directed by Sorious Samura which will be aired on CNN. Sorious Samura is an award winning Sierra Leonean journalist who is best known for two other documentary hits: "Cry Freetown" (2000) and "Exodus from Africa" (2001). He has two other very recent documentaries "Living with Hunger" and "Living with Refugees" which has been nominated for an Emmy award.

Why am I talking about Blood Diamonds in a blog about Antigua and Barbuda?

I see parallels between those who would ferment and encourage civil war and violence in Africa so that they can enrich themselves in the mega companies in their mega countries making mega bucks – and those who would ferment political and social divisiveness in Antigua and Barbuda so that they can entrench themselves here in their mega family owned companies, coming from both mega countries and meager backgrounds in order to make mega bucks.

I see parallels between the evil piratical activities of the executives of the companies who profit from blood diamonds and those who seek to profit through piratical activities in the Caribbean whether they own banks, airlines, big stores, or car companies.

I see parallels between those who stuff the pockets of African opposition leaders and political operatives with millions of dollars and those stuff the pockets of Caribbean leaders – political and social – famous and infamous – with blood money. (Not only stuffing their pockets but tantalizing them and in so doing tarnishing their good names... some of them with world famous names!)

I see parallels between those international speculators who see diamonds as a way to enrich themselves by stealing (by any means necessary) the diamonds that belong to the people of Africa... and those international speculators in Antigua and Barbuda and other

Caribbean countries who see our beautiful beaches and our pristine coastlines as a way to further enrich themselves through bribery and clandestine illegal deals.

I see parallels between those piratical investors in blood diamonds who show no respect for the wealth that belongs to the African peoples and those piratical Caribbean investors who totally disregard the fact that the beaches are ours, the islands are ours, the land is ours... not matter how much money they have to fling around.

I see many more parallels... but I think you understand where I am coming from. What should we do?

We need to fight these blood diamond type speculators and investors with everything that we have. We have to deny them the power of their money. We have to neutralize the evil influence that they have on our social, religious and political leaders.

We have to rid ourselves of them and of the 'politicocrats' and bureaucrats who menace our future., and who will use their ill-gotten 'blood' monies to finance their thirst for future power and immediate wealth.

Yes, we need to fight those among us and the forces within us which allow us to be susceptible to their inducements and manipulation.

How Do We Get Out of This Mess?

February 2007

WHAT MESS? OUR 'economic' mess... our 'lack of development' mess... our 'can't pay the workers' mess... our 'no new industries' mess... our 'unemployment' mess... our 'underemployment' mess... our 'bottom-less indebtedness' mess... our 'politicians corruption' mess...

So... pick one!

The answer does not lie with UP-P. The answer does not lie with AL-P. The answer does not lie with Baldwin Spencer. The answer does not lie with Lester Bird. And the answer certainly does not lie with any of their cohorts.

At least... the answer does not lie with any one party or person.

The answer does not lie with the Chamber of Commerce. The answer does not lie with the Employers Federation. The answer does not lie with the Trade Union Congress. The answer does not lie with the Christian Council.

The answer does not lie with any select group.

The answer does not lie with any one online pundit... or radio personality... or sports figure... or church leader... or grass roots organizer.

The answer does not lie with giving away our lands to modern day pirates of the Caribbean. The answer does not lie with begging for handouts from former colonial slave masters. The answer does not lie with pleading for support from capitalism's core – America.

And the answer certainly does not lie with those who are fostering ties to the Japanese, Lebanese or the 22nd Century's colonialists – the Chinese!

And let's be clear... the answer doesn't lie in begging for money from the organizations located on American streets... neither Washington's K Street or 16th Street, or New York's Wall Street. And we certainly should not want to deal with those colonizing crooks from the International Development Bank or the World Bank...

So where is the answer?

Let's start right here in Antigua.

We don't need partisan politics. It doesn't work at least not for the vast majority of Antiguans. As a matter of fact it doesn't work anywhere in the Caribbean, Africa or any other developing nation. (I don't think it works anywhere.) We don't need partisan leaders. We don't need partisan followers. We don't need a blue party, or a red party, or a green party, or a democratic party or a republican party...

We need every single Antiguan – (and those want-to-be Antiguans too) – to commit themselves to one vision and to one set of goals and one party – The Antigua Party! (Barbuda should get its own! But that's for another article.)

We need UPP, ALP (and all the other P's) to commit to lead as one... under one umbrella. Forget so called party type democracy... it is splitting this country (and every other country in the world) apart. It has split our people apart!

We need Spencer and Lester and every politically aspiring leader to join together under a unanimous umbrella to lead our nation out of this mess. As a matter of fact we don't need a UPP Tent – we need an Antiguan Tent!

We need the unions, the churches, the business organizations, the pundits, and the media to come together with a common mission... a common understanding... that we must pull our country out, and up and away from this economic morass.

So, what is the vision? What is the mission? What is the goal?

It would be presumptive of me to determine that. I have my own opinion... But all parties should come together... All the people should come together... to determine the way forward... to determine the one core... the central vision for our nation. And then every person in this nation should buy-in and commit to this core vision and mission.

First we start with the politicians putting down their swords and shields... Putting away their manifestos... Putting away their partisan positions... and certainly putting aside their individual aspirations to be 'the big man'.

I think that the latter will be the most difficult to accomplish... Many of those aspirants have waited long in the wings... waited for their turn (just like this UPP bunch has). Now they smell their opportunity... and are ready to pounce... And guess what... the people will suffer. Partisan politics all over again. Five more years... and five more... of the same foolishness... with different faces! Different decision makers... same results... different corrupt officials... different hat-in-the-hand beggar-leaders!

There is a saying that if you do what you always did... you will get what you always got! And of course, many of you know that Einstein is attributed with saying that the definition of insanity is that you keep doing the same thing and keep expecting a different result...

We elect a party... they win another election... and another... and we keep getting the same thing over and over. Then, by some miracle, we elect another party... with great hype... promises of sunshine... and... to quote a new book: "Oh Gad", they fall into the same old same old... and we... get the same old, same old results.

But I digress. (My own wounds of hurt, disappointment and sense of betrayal by so-called leaders of the people are deep and cut to the heart...) But I – we must look to the big picture.

How can we get out of this mess?

We need to change this political merry-go-round! I will not be part of electing another party... for another five years of corruption, poor decision making, poor leadership, management incompetence, arrogance and just plain foolishness... while people continue to suffer – even as they hope for better.

Now... that may be a bit harsh... but it is the reality. We can do better... if every brain... every brawn.. every talent... be brought under our flag... one strategic vision... to lift the nation. We can do it.

We need new and visionary leadership... coupled with the wisdom of those who have the experience... coupled with those who have the expertise. We need leadership not of a party... not from a party... but leadership that is able to pull all Antiguans together... on one mission...

How can we get novel, creative, world class, innovative solutions to our problems?

The answer to that is that we need talented, skilled, knowledgeable, creative, committed and innovative minds and bodies that are focused on success for all...

Do we have them?

My answer to that is an unequivocal yes!

Well... where are they?

First... I can tell you where they are not! They are not in Cabinet. They are not in the Senate. They are not in the House! (And if, by chance some of them are talented, skilled or knowledgeable... they are hampered by something... ego... arrogance... maybe by their personal agenda or the party machine and propaganda... or by their corrupt mentality.)

So where are our talented, skilled, knowledgeable, creative, committed focused and innovative minds and bodies? They are sitting behind Public and Private Sector desks. Some have degrees... some just their CXCs... But they all have one problem: They are stymied by a system that does not allow the cream to come to top!

And The World Watches...
Silently... Still!

January, 2007

I HAVE HAD it. I have been silent too long. For too long I have watched without saying anything.

Enough is enough.

The world watches... silently as Israel destroys Palestine. The world watches silently as Israel kills children, mothers, grandmothers and great grandfathers. The world watches silently.

World leaders – all of them – are afraid to raise a voice against Israel. World leaders – cowardly – all of them – afraid to confront the genocidal Israeli aggression against the people of Palestine.

Leaders everywhere... cowardly... silent...

And why? Hamas, they say, started the current situation by firing a few missiles against Israel... killing a handful of Israelis. And for that, Israel, in return kills thousands of Palestinian men, women and children and wounds thousands more. Israel destroys schools, hospitals, apartment buildings and Palestinian infrastructure.

And why? Because Israel senses a change in the air. A new administration is entering Washington, and Israel is uncertain of how the new president will really respond to the one-sided power play in the mid-east. And so, using Hamas' stupid and folly attack they respond with all their might.

Israel, the only nuclear power in the region, receiving billions of U.S. dollars of military aid every year, receiving the best of America's military weaponry – uses it against poor people who can scarcely afford food.

Over the years, I have noticed that the world seems to put more value on a few Israeli lives than hundreds of Palestinian lives. A Palestinian suicide bomber creates havoc in an Israeli town and kills ten Israelis. Israel responds by unleashing its military might and kills five hundred Palestinian. One Israeli child dies... world leaders respond with outrage. Fifteen Palestinian children die... those same leaders are silent.

They say... like Bush and Rice said recently... that Israel has a right to defend itself. OK. So what about the Palestinians? I guess they have no rights at all. No rights to defend their lands stolen first by the British and given to Israel. And then perpetually being stolen and carved up by Israel for the Jewish immigrants they import from around the world.

I don't care how old this issue is... these are modern times. You cannot steal my land and say it belonged to your ancestors ten thousand years ago. All people everywhere have a right to defend their land.

And the world watches and is silent as Israel steals the land and kills the owners... and the children of the owners. As a matter of fact the world does not only watch... they help Israel to perpetrate these heinous acts... not only with their silence... but with the moneys and weapons that they give to Israel every year.

I cannot perceive anything more terrifying than hearing the monstrous roar of 20 of the world's most sophisticated and technologically capable warplanes rolling through the skies dropping bombs at will without my people having any chance to defend ourselves.

I cannot perceive anything more terrible than having tanks roll across the soccer fields of my schools and down the alleys of my communities belching exploding rockets into our schools, mosques and hospitals.

I cannot perceive anything more terrorist-like than seeing our babies being blown up in their cribs, seeing our young children with their legs blown off, and seeing our elderly dying at the sides of our streets.

I cannot perceive a feeling of being more helpless that I cannot respond... that I have no war planes to fight back with... that I have no tanks to roll out and confront the enemy...

I cannot perceive how it feels to know... that no one cares... that all the other nations... even my Muslim brother and sister nations... are silent...

Israel... a country... a people who ought to know better because of what they endured more than sixty years ago. Israel... now... today... they are the perpetrators of genocide... and the world is as silent now as it was when it was perpetrated against them.

And, why is the world afraid of Israel? That answer is for another day.

Today... I am not afraid of you. But the rest of the world is.

And, our moral leaders... religious leaders... are like all those others. Afraid to raise their voices publicly.

I have had it. I have been silent too long. I have watched too long... silently. Enough is enough.

Is Capitalism Now A Threat to America?

February 2007

YES! CAPITALISM IS now a threat to America!

How did I come to that conclusion? To answer that question allow me to set the stage by explaining how capitalism is generally defined.

Adam Smith in his 1776 book, "The Wealth of Nations" popularized the economic theory which we now call 'capitalism'. According to economists, "capitalism is an economic system based on private ownership of the means of producing goods and providing services." 'Private owners' invest in the enterprise, control the system of production and therefore reap the profits or share the losses. Capitalism is typically characterized by competition in a 'free market' system and is driven solely by 'the profit motive'.

Other characteristics which are associated with capitalism include notions of 'free enterprise' and a 'free market regulated by supply and demand'. Contemporary capitalism is often analyzed in three sectors: industry (e.g. manufacture, technology), services (retail, administration, professional) and finance (banking, stock markets).

The one defining characteristic of capitalism is the notion of the **'profit motive'**. In economic terms, this is where privately owned enterprises are free to make as much profit as they can, given certain market conditions. The profit motive is regarded by capitalists to be a good thing.

I have outlined in other articles my personal objection to the notion that the profit motive as defined above is a 'good thing'!

And that is where I rejoin the core position of this short article: Capitalism is now a threat to America... and the rest of the world.

Let's focus on America and take a good look at the evidence. American companies are fleeing America in droves. And even when they stay in America... they register their companies overseas in companies where they pay little or no tax.

Companies are outsourcing work to China, Mexico, Brazil, Thailand – anywhere where they can pay less for labor and less taxes.

Companies are outsourcing jobs in all three of the sectors mentioned above particularly in the areas of industry (manufacturing and technology jobs) and service (customer, administrative and technical services). According to a labor expert at Cornell's School of Industrial and Labor Relations, 48,417 U.S. jobs were outsourced to other countries or were publicly announced as being scheduled for outsourcing, from January through March 2004 (a 3 month period!!!). Of the documented jobs that left the United States for other countries in January through March 2004, 23,396 went to Mexico, 8,283 to China, 3,895 to India, 5,511 to Latin American countries other than Mexico, 4,419 to Asian countries other than China and 2,933 to other countries.

It is now thought that in 2006, America might be losing over 25,000 jobs *each month* to global outsourcing – and this is thought to be a conservative estimate!

So which companies are outsourcing? There is not enough space in this article to list them. But here are a few 'All American Companies": Aetna, Amazon.com, AT&T, Apple, Bank of America, Boeing, Charles Schwab, DuPont, Ford, General Motors, Goodyear, Google, Kodak, ExxonMobil, General Electric, IBM, Intel, Microsoft, Motorola, Nike, Quaker Oats, Sprint, Target, Verizon, Xerox, and Yahoo. Yes... the biggest and richest American-as-apple-pie companies now build their products elsewhere and export them back to America!!

And, why are these companies outsourcing their work to the rest of the world? There is one answer: *The profit motive.*

Labor in America costs more than labor in Mexico, China or India! Experts say that the major reason that companies outsource is because they can lower their costs of operation (production or service). When companies outsource they are able to control their budget, focus their supplier on cost and quality, and depend less on internal resources. They also don't have to pay attention to overheads like staff insurance and employee leave and vacation costs. And they don't have to negotiate with labor unions!

The bottom line is that it costs less to operate when they out-source... and therefore companies make more profit! Capitalism is the system where private owners invest their 'capital' in ways that allow them to make as much profit as possible. Therefore, compa-nies that outsource globally are fully applying the principles of this American and Eurocentric economic system called capitalism.

So, what's wrong with outsourcing globally?

When America loses more than 25,000 jobs each month, the every-day lives of ordinary Americans will be seriously impacted. People are losing their jobs and they are not finding work to replace their income. This is having a huge impact on many other sectors in the economy and having a disastrous consequence on the individual lives of people. One example of this is the fact that the foreclosure rate all across America has exploded. In November, 2006, it was reported, for example, that the foreclosure rate in Georgia jumped 99% over one year! In some markets, foreclosures had gone up 300%, while nation-ally foreclosures were up 43%.

When jobs go overseas, homeowners can't pay their mortgage. These people will lose their homes soon after they lose their jobs. When they lose their jobs, they can't pay their kids school fees; they can't pay their bills; their ability to buy food is diminished; they can't pay for medical care; they can't pay to train themselves to get new job skills. When jobs go overseas to China or across the border to Mexico, people have less to spend on the very same products that are sent back to America.

The movement of jobs from America to other countries has left the American worker in dire straits and there is evidence that this has had negative impacts on the society: Crime has increased in formally stable areas like Detroit and Pittsburg. Drug and alcohol use have increased exponentially. Homelessness has gone up. Mental health diagnoses such as depression, suicidal tendencies, and anxiety disorders have increased. Heart attacks and other health problems related to increased stress and cynicism have skyrocketed.

In addition to all of that, here is the major problem: Those jobs are not coming back. Why?

Because those companies who have emigrated to places like Mexico and China have experienced the holy grail of capitalism: increased profits at lower costs with increased shareholder value and obscene wages for those in corporate boardrooms!

Like any addict – they will never relinquish the drug of capital globalization. Why not?

Because there have been not consequences for their exodus from their homeland and their betrayal of their country. If you do a Google search on the impact of globalization, you will notice that 99% of the articles ignore the price that the ordinary person pays for the desertion of the American company from its people.

Capitalism and its latest incarnation – globalization – is not only a threat to America. It is a threat that has come to fruition.

New Sidewalks!

March 2007

MY MOTHER IS now singing the praises of the UPP government. Why? Because at 92, when she goes to shop in St. Johns, she can walk along the sidewalks without fear of being hit by a car. She likes the wider, flatter and lower sidewalks. The only things she says that she has to look out for are those red painted, poorly designed grates. She says that the bars should be placed closer together. But, she is not really complaining too much.

So... she is both thankful and surprised.

Why surprised? Well... the sidewalks and the road improvements were not there the last time she walked through the city. She is amazed at the speed with which the project is being completed. She is further amazed, because in Antigua, it is highly unusual for projects... particularly public sector projects... especially public projects conducted by Public Works... to be done quickly. And when you add... efficiently, effectively and attractively... well that is historically unheard of.

Now she knows that Public Works had help. She knows that the Cubans seemed to have put us to shame and that that might have provided the necessary prick on our pride to spur our Public Works' staff to respond positively to the challenge.

And respond they have... and well... so far – so good.

But, truth be told, the stronger prick and push came not from the Cubans but from the imminent arrival of Cricket World Cup.

For months... maybe longer... just about everyone in the country have been fussing about the need to fix the roads... all roads. Even some Ministers of the current Government seemed to have been discontented with the situation. There were charges from some elected officials that the Ministry of Finance were not releasing the money for public projects. There were counter charges that Public Works was not providing the proper documentation to request the necessary funds. There were even charges that one Minister who controlled the purse strings was making a 'power play'!

But all of the squabbling dissipated when everyone realized that the opening date for CWC was just around the corner! There was a deadline. There was no getting around it. There was no getting away from it. The date was set in stone. So the stones had to be worked. And so, what needed to be done was done – quickly. And the city is being transformed. As an aside, the question is – how well were the stones put together... and how long will they last? They look good – but...!

So it took the imminent arrival of CWC to drive our Government to implement this project of upgrading the city. According to a local DJ and radio personality with a snake name, it seems as though we need to bring CWC here to Antigua every month in order for Government to complete all of the projects that it has promised.

Sad... but true.

So... what other events might we the people highlight that would get a similar response from the Government? How can we get the Government to fix all the roads and alleys? How can we influence them, or push them to really make significant adjustments to the airport? What can we do to get them to implement serious programming to address the apparently high levels of crime and violence? What kind of pricking is needed to have them foster deep and lasting improvements to our education system?

And what do we have to do to get any Government... UPP or who-ever... to continuously deliver on the projects that they promise?

Elections? Maybe we should have elections more often. First, I think that we need to change from an appointed Senate to an elected one. Then we need to change elections for the Lower House from every five years to every three years. The Senate would also be elected every three years. Both elections would be held on alternate years. So, for example, the next election for the Lower House would be held in 2008 (and every three years thereafter), and the elections for our new Senate would be held in 2009 (and every three years thereafter.)

That would keep politicians hopping. That would keep them delivering. And, we the people would see a never ending stream of projects – creatively, efficiently, effectively and attractively done – just like the sidewalks in St. Johns.

By the way... My mother wants to know: "Why were the grates painted **red**?"

American Interests

April 2007

MSNBC CABLE TELEVISION evening shows sometimes provide good coverage of news *and* views. The hosts often give broad
and varying perspectives that often allow viewers to sift through
where fact and fiction depart.

I particularly liked Keith Olbermann's Countdown where he pas-
sionately commented on the shenanigans of America's right wing
conservative politicians. I also highly appreciated Chris Matthews
Hardball where he asks tough questions that CNN and Fox News
often avoid. Tucker Carlson in my mind is a misfit in the line-up. But I
guess he brings some balance as he desperately tries to find his niche
as a newbie-conservative... at least that's what I call him.

Joe Scarborough of Scarborough Country appears to be another
conservative... at least he is a former Republican Congressman from
Florida. I noticed how he often shifts his perspectives on how the
Bush Government mishandled the Katrina hurricane and turned a
disaster into a debacle, tragedy, mess and catastrophe all rolled into
one.

I used to think that his views on Iraq were similarly balanced. But
last week, Joe Scarborough made a couple of statements that have
thrown me into a deep introspective and inner self discussion about
a lofty subject... world peace.

Scarborough was discussing the Iraq quagmire with some of his guests. At the end of the discussion he stated that he wants America to win in Iraq. Good enough. Although, he was not clear about *what* he wanted America to win and what winning meant. But it was his second statement that threw me for a loop.

Joe Scarborough said that he was **not** interested in world peace... he wanted whatever was good for America and for **America's interest.** **He was not interested in world peace... only in whatever was in America's interest.**

That statement finally explained a lot of things that have puzzled me for years about the difference between what American leaders say... and what they do.

Every single American act on the world stage demonstrates that its leaders are less interested in a democratic world and more interested in a world that bows to American interests.

So, in Palestine the people chose Hamas in free and fair elections... but of course that choice is not in America's so-called interest. In Venezuela, the people chose Chavez, and of course, that is not in America's stated interest. In Bolivia, the people chose Evo Morales, and of course, that is not in America's identified interest.

In each of these countries one sees the best evidence of 'democracy' in action. And in each case, the so-called champion of democracy, America, was critical of the results. Why? Because none of these winners were the ones supported by the American political establishment (including Democrats and Republicans).

American leaders are less interested in people who are free to choose whatever they want to choose and more interested in people who choose to allow Americans to tell them what to choose and whom to elect.

Uncomfortably Comfortable

January 5ᵗʰ 2009

LAST EVENING I attended the commissioning of the new UPP headquarters. Reportedly there was a massive crowd! Why reportedly when I was right there? Well it is hard to tell the size of crowds when the people are tightly packed on a narrow road in a small area. The claim was that the road was packed solid for over two blocks! However, because I was standing in one place for the duration of the activity – I really cannot ascertain the claim. At best, it was a large crowd cooped 'upp' in a small area.

In any case there were many issues with which I was uncomfortable… some decidedly made me warm under the collar. The first issue was the fact that UPP imported a band – all the way from Jamaica, the Fab 5, to play for the event. Why was the UPP so willing to spend the kind of money that they obviously did in order to have this band from Jamaica? Is it that we don't have any quality bands in Antigua that could have done as well or better? Or, is it that all of the quality bands or already committed to the other party?

Another issue was the fact that although there were a number of religious 'acts' and two Bishops– none of them really said or did anything that I think remotely suggested that this was a dedication or ceremonial opening of a new headquarters. In truth, throughout the evening no one, not the 'hidden' mysterious voice that seemed at times to be playing the role of the Mistress of Ceremonies, not even the Prime Minister, paid much attention, if any, to why we were invited to this event! As far as I can recall, the Bishops did not bless the place. The mysterious 'Honourable' Mistress of Ceremonies who I can't remember being introduced, or introducing herself by name, did not much reference the building, or the new office, or 'election command center'.

And then there is the matter of the building itself. I was very uncomfortable with whom it is rented from. I groaned when I heard the name of the owner. Here we go again: Same family. Different part of the tree? Same name! Here we go again! I wonder who engineered that pathetic stroke of un-genius.

Of course, there was the issue of the obviously missing parliamentary representative. The Prime Minister claims that he was absent because his wife had taken ill. There is much that can be said – but of course all of that would be feeding the rampant speculation. The least that I can say is that his absence was profoundly curious! He was missed only to the effect that the numbers did not add up... I kept saying one is missing... one is missing... Then it dawned on me who the one was... And for that reason the excuse did not add up either. As a matter of fact two were missing... the representative from Barbuda for whatever reason was not there... At least... he was not introduced to us and no excuse was given for his absence.

The core of my discomfort, however, was centered on all the accolades and dramatic tributes that were heaped on the Prime Minister before his presentation. Most of Fab 5's songs featured the Honorable Prime Minister and the introduction read by the well known voice of the 'hidden' and mysterious un-named Mistress of Ceremonies that heaped praises and compliments on him. And then there was the love song that one of the featured singers sang for him as he stood there listening and apparently uncomfortably and nervously fidgeting... "Everything I do, I do it for you"! I certainly like the lyrics "Take me as I am - take my life - I would give it all - I would sacrifice" as a testimony for this once giant figure from Rural West. But I am distinctly uncomfortable when a party elevates an individual above the party.

Last night was not about the building or the command center. Last night was not about the members of the UPP election team. Last night was not even about the UPP. As a matter of fact – even the Chairman of the party was missing from the program. Last night was not about the supporters of the UPP. Last night was not about the opposition. Last night was not even about the pending election.

Last night appeared to be about Baldwin Spencer. And for that reason I was uncomfortably comfortable.

I was and continue to be distinctly uncomfortable that UPP finds itself in a position where it has to highlight the party leader rather than put the major emphasis on the party and its other candidates. The Baldwin Spencer that I used to know would have been uncomfortable with this. As a matter of fact Baldwin Spencer did appear uncomfortable. In his own words, at the microphone, he said "Wow, this feels like a coronation." And a coronation it appeared to be!

Yes, last night I was squirming in my shoes. Not that he does not deserve the accolades for efforts of the past 25 five years – particularly the earlier years (before his first inauguration). Not that he does not deserve the tributes for decades of past service to his constituency. But this is not about Baldwin Spencer. The situation we find ourselves in as a nation is millions of times bigger than any one personality.

But... I also saw the necessity. I saw several psychological and practical reasons for the attempt at a new 'coronation'. I more than saw the necessity... I was comfortable with the fact that it was attempted. I was more than comfortable... For a few moments I leaned towards supporting it... even in my discomfort.

First of all, in politics as in most anything else that involves human beings, the cult of the individual deity or leader is paramount. Whether it be Krishna, Yahwe, Allah or the Christian God. Whether it be Jesus, Mohammed or Buddha. Whether it be Napoleon, George Washington, Kennedy, Gandhi, Martin Luther King, Hitler, Fidel Castro, or Mandela. Or whether it be George Walter, V.C. Bird, Barack Obama or Baldwin Spencer. The cult of the individual leader works. And sometimes works well. And it seems to work particularly well when the party is faced with serious opposition on various fronts.

In the current situation, UPP is faced with opposition on several fronts. On one front is the obvious opposition from the ALP. I say obvious but by no means do I imply trivial. The ALP led by Lester Bird is a force to be reckoned with. On another front there are of course the want-to-be parties that are nibbling at the heels of the two major parties. They, at this moment in time, are inconsequential.

Less obvious but definitely significant are the not so hidden forces of the moneyed who are attempting to hijack the democratic process by reportedly sliding millions of dollars into the coffers of individual candidates of both major parties – to destroy from within and/or from without.

So what does all this have to do with my being uncomfortably comfortable? And specifically why am I comfortable with last night's focus on Baldwin Spencer? Well... it is rumored that key individuals of the moneyed class are trying to fund and buy Mr. Spencer's demise... either to have him lose his seat or more demonically... to have him lose the support of the candidates that he currently will lead into the elections. What does this mean? It means that if UPP wins, the moneyed pirates of Antigua, would like to see a UPP parliamentarian – one who used to be in inner circle of the ALP – uplifted to the leadership of the government and replace Mr. Spencer.

So... in my mind, last night was an attempt by those in the party who continue to support the Prime Minister to send a strong message not only to the electorate, but to his not-so-hidden detractors within his own Cabinet. The message says that Baldwin Spencer is the leader of the party. Baldwin Spencer is the people's champion. Baldwin Spencer is the conscience of the UPP. Baldwin Spencer represents the roots of the party. Baldwin Spencer represents the common folk of the party. Baldwin Spencer is the people's choice to continue to lead the party into the future.

Last night was a warning to those who would usurp the leadership that no just-come turn-'coat' politician who was part of the problem in the past can come into this – from that – and take over. It is a warning to those who 'court' the favors of millionaires and who themselves have benefitted millions for <u>court</u>-ing millionaires, and who have not paid their dues by <u>court</u>-ing the people of Antigua and Barbuda cannot and will not be allowed to connive against the natural leader of the country.

Those within the UPP courtyard, who court the American millionaire pirate, who court the middle-eastern pirate family, who court the worst inclinations of their parliamentary colleagues, who have continuously clandestinely undermined and stymied the financial decisions of the Prime Minister, and who have done so at home and abroad, should take warning. Take heed.

Last night was also a warning to those others who have become rich in five years – not from the ministerial or parliamentary representative salaries – that they should tread cautiously. None of them on that stage last night received any particularly noticeable response from the people. As a matter of fact, with the exception of the candidate from City South, most of the responses were tepid... at best. The crowd reserved their accolades for the man of the night. Their livelihood and their lifestyles, continue to be at the whim and fancy of the common folk... enabled, maintained and perpetuated through the people's champion.

So last night the crowd gave tribute to the Prime Minister through their vociferous cheering. They indicated that they approve of him and that they support him.

I did too – even though I too am becoming increasingly uncomfortably uncomfortable with that notion.

The "Clausification" of Antigua and the Caribbean

- US$35 Million 'loan' to LIAT
- US$25 Million for West Indies cricket.
- EC$25 Million for a special school.
- US$1+ Million for the public library.
- EC$100,000 for select politicians in Antigua… and maybe elsewhere. And that is the amount that is above the table…
- US$ Millions for selected political parties… not only in Antigua…
- US$ Millions for the Antigua airport.

THE PEOPLE OF Antigua and Barbuda and those in many other Caribbean nations just like other people in countries all over the world look forward to those special times in the year when gifts are exchanged. Some people look forward to gifts even though they can't give any in return. And in many cases, there is always some agency or some kind and loving person who care enough to lovingly share with those who are less fortunate. Santa Claus is one familiar, albeit fake, gift giver who is known worldwide.

According to Wikipedia, Santa is a symbolic gift-giving person, who is based on the real life and historical figure of Saint Nicholas. Santa Claus is an 'eminent' character in the hearts and minds of millions of children and adults around the world who 'believe' in him. Some historians claim that Santa Claus is a variation of a Dutch folk tale of the bishop (Saint Nicholas) who used his whole inheritance to assist the needy, the sick and the suffering.

As almost everyone can see, these days millions of dollars are being showered on Antigua and Barbuda, on West Indies Cricket and have been floated among many of our countries in the region. We seem to have found a modern day, real life Santa Claus.

I think that our local and regional Claus --- Stanta Claus --- has started a Machiavellian process where the money that is being showered and floated in Antigua and the rest of the Caribbean will cause the development of an addiction, a dependence, a reliance on Stanta Claus' money.

We in these small countries have only just come out of a forced 'dependence' on Great Britain. As a matter of fact... we really are not fully independent – not politically, not economically and not financially. And, even worse, I think that are still dependent – psychologically.

We are still looking for England, America, or the World Bank to prop us up. In their absence... we have always looked to individual Santa Clauses to get from and 'exchange' gifts with. The only problem is that these modern day Clauses always get the lion share of any deal... whether it is the notion of an Asian Village, electricity power deals, giving away airport lands or doling out our coastal islands.

This danger is multiplied when one realizes that we have 'Clausified' our economy: Huge salaries being paid to a few executives in the local Stanta Claus' company; ordinary laborers making being paid higher wages than teachers; and, people being hired to fritter around buildings and lawns without doing any real work.

Then, these people make decisions to build homes and send their children to college based on their anomalous Stanta Claus' salaries.

And then, woe and lo and behold, many of them are dismissed and just fired outright!

The money that is being flashed around will boost the economy. And apparently it has. But then when it is taken away – as has been threatened by Father Stanta, we will have become dependent – like an addict without his fix.

I maintain that we are already addicted: Politicians who go with their palms opened wide... promising everything to Stanta; Competent, highly trained, qualified business technocrats have left jobs where they were making valuable contributions to the nation. One very top and prominent public sector executive with years of service left his high profile public sector job with the brag... "It's my time now!" I guess it was his time to get paid! But some of them, having put themselves at the mercy of Stanta, have already been forced out or kicked out.

You know that things are bad when even the Catholic Church has to go basket in hand and gets its coffers buttressed and blessed by Stanta Claus!

We are in serious danger. The threat posed by Clausification is real. We will find ourselves at the mercy of this 'gifter'. There is definitely some evil afoot... some skeleton in the closet... some macabre master plan... But no one is looking too hard... Money blinds even the best of us. Money hides evil. And in this case... lots of money are being spread around!

It is interesting to note that not everyone accepts that the origin of Santa Claus started with St. Nicholas. There are a number of Christians who 'even claim that Santa is a hidden representation of Satan. Notice that 'Santa' and 'Satan' contain the same letters! Some people point to the close resemblance of "Santa Claus" to "Satan's Claws". (All of these letters – S, T, A, and N... need to be closely looked at. Do you know any modern day 'Santa Claus' in the Caribbean with those letters in their names?)

I do believe that here in the Caribbean, our 'Clausification' means that we have allowed ourselves to be gripped in a modern day version of "Satan's Claws". I hope and pray that I am wrong.

I am deeply worried that one day, we will awake and realize that we are in the grip of a monstrous entity from which we cannot find financial, economic, or spiritual release or relief.

Why? Because we have been Stanta Clausified and it is going to haunt us for years to come!

Can You Feel It?

January, 2010

I WAS RECENTLY on a Southwest Airlines flight from Houston to Baltimore. We left Houston about forty minutes late and the pilot promised to make up some time on the normally three hours long flight. When he said that I knew that he meant that he intended to go faster than the speed limit! On Southwest Airlines, that is typical... their mentality is the reverse of well... LIAT. They strive to be always on time!

When we left Houston it was cold and rainy. About an hour into the flight... the seat belt light came on... and the pilot advised us that there was turbulence ahead. He was right!

Turbulence... that is not descriptive enough! It was rough. Up... down... sideways... Going up... going up... drop! Twist to the right... drop... twist to the left - bounce up! It was awful...

I looked around. People had the reading lights above their seats on. A couple of people were on their computers... Of course every now and then the computers would levitate and then slap back down to the seat-back tables while their fingers remained suspended in the air. Some people were reading... while others appeared to be sleeping!

That bumpy ride continued on and off for about an hour. When we thought that we had patched through to calmer skies... the bucking would start again.

But I couldn't understand the calmness of the people! Then it hit me... This was Texas... Cowboys and rodeo riders! They were accustomed to wild rides on bucking horse and snorting bulls!

Of course that was not it. You see... I left out one detail. Every ten minutes or so... the captain would announce how much longer he thought we would be enduring this ride... and of course he got it wrong several times... and each time he would come back on and give us an update. "There are several planes ahead of us... and they are reporting that the turbulence will continue for just a little longer!"

The flight attendants did their part. The captain had instructed them to remain seated and buckled in! Yet, every now and then they would get up... hold on to the seats... and go down the aisle to rub a shoulder... make an encouraging remark to a crying toddler... the kinds of stuff that you don't see on American Airlines... But then this is Southwest Airlines well known for singing, dancing, comedic flight attendants and pilots!

On this night, we could feel the pilot's presence. We felt his efforts to keep the plane stable. He kept connected to us. He gave us regular updates. He made a few light-hearted remarks. He updated us on the weather in Baltimore. He told us that although we were having a rough ride - that we would eventually reach Baltimore only fifteen minutes later than scheduled (Meaning that he was still breaking the speed limit!). He told us what the weather in Baltimore was.. and even commented on a major basketball game that was currently being played (people applauded when they heard the score!).

Eventually, the ride smoothed out... and we did land in Baltimore at the time he had indicated.

The ride was bumpy... turbulent... but it wasn't frightening. Why? Because of the leadership of the pilot. We felt his presence. We felt the presence of his team. He kept us informed about current events. He kept us connected to our destination... He stayed connected to us!

I felt him... I felt his control over the situation... I wasn't overly concerned... This guy and his team were in full control over the situation!

Here are my questions to you, as we think of Antigua and Barbuda - can you feel it?

Things are bumpy now. High levels of crime and a depressing economic situation are only two of the many deep problems we have! But, can you feel the Captain and his team? What's the plan? Do you know where we are going? Do you know how we are going to get there? Do you think we are given timely updates? Do you have a sense of how things are going? Do you feel safe and secure? Are we in good hands? Are you worried?

Can you feel it?

The Pope, The President & The PM

April, 2010

FOR THE LAST ten years I have been seriously disenchanted with the Catholic Church. Well... to tell the truth, I have always been disenchanted with the Church for its role in slavery and its sordid history on tens of other matters affecting people around the globe.

But these last ten years or so have been painful as case after case after case sexual abuse of children by priests in every corner of the globe have been brought from the pits of hell into the light of day.

And one thing that has turned the screws into my pain has been the Catholic Church's response: Denials; Moving priests around (giving them access to more children to abuse); Paying off parents to keep quiet; Blaming reporters for reporting these vile acts; In reality... protecting those who violate the vulnerable and unprotected... The list of the Church's poor responses goes on.

And now... the Pope... even he is now reportedly implicated in improperly handling a case (or cases) of these vile priests when he was bishop or archbishop or whatever...

Today, April 2nd, Good Friday, two days before Easter Sunday, the response of the Vatican is to target and object to reporters who report on these criminal priests and those who protect them.

Internationally, the general public has been outraged... people continue to be aghast at the depths of depravity wrought on the innocent by these so-called 'holy men'!

For a while, it seemed as though all of the cases of abuse by priests had been reported... But now... everyday... almost everywhere, more victims are finding the courage to speak up. And the outrage around the world is growing...

And ordinary Catholics have been silent... I guess that they are afraid of being excommunicated. The Catholics I know don't talk about this subject. They avoid the issue.

The Vatican, the political center of the Catholic world, has wanted to be silent, to be above the fray, too holy to respond... But because of the fact that the pope himself has been touched, they have recently come out with a wimpish attempt at responding...

It is too little – too late. This issue could well balloon to such a degree that it might well place the papacy in a constitutional crisis. And it might well place the pope in a position where his leadership is undermined and put in question!

Constitutional crisis? Leadership threatened? Yep!

And it didn't have to happen.

The leadership (of the Church) should have addressed the issues (years ago) by forthrightly denouncing these criminal priests. The leadership (of the Church) should have searched for, exposed and rooted out these wolves who preyed on the lambs in its flock. The leadership (of the Church) should have been at the forefront rather than at the backend of this issue.

Leadership is about stepping out in front of issues. Leadership is about responding to the concerns of the people. Leadership is about working for and on behalf of the members or followers.

A good example of this type of leadership is being shown by President Obama. He has stepped out in front of the issue of healthcare. The buck stops with him. He is the primary spokes person. He has taken full responsibility for its success or failure.

And yes... there is a lot of opposition. In the face of such opposition, he didn't run and hide behind pundits and surrogates. He stepped out in front and took the poll and political hits that were thrown at him.

Leaders cannot choose to speak only when the stuff has hit the fan!

Leaders who choose to be silent amidst the crescendo of popular discourse and disharmony, are leaders who stand the risk of being swept away by the upheavals of discord.

Leaders who choose to be silent, who choose to be non-responsive, who choose to let others talk for them, are leaders who risk being former leaders!

This is the case whether the leader is a pope, a president or ... a prime minister!

My Tears

November, 2010

"Scottie! What's up?" I shout as I drive slowly past.
"Misser Mutley!" "Teacha!" were shouts I heard in return,
From men sitting at the corner – most of them with heads downcast...
Men who look older than their age... nothing to do... only time to
burn.

And as I drive by, another car, a black SUV passes me.
Dark tinted windows, special plates, the occupant hidden.
The men shout out a name... Their shouts reflecting both hope and
futility...
As the black vehicle speeds up... deepening the sadness of those
downtrodden.

Everyday... every night, these men are on Skem's corner.
Men who I knew when they were kids and teens –
I was their teacher, soccer coach, unofficial counselor...
"Me nar work" is their cry now – an answer that is routine, as it
demeans.

Most of the kids (or grand kids) of these men are at another site,
A hundred yards or so away, close to that Tinning Village supermarket.

They too sit around, gambling, smoking or getting into fights...
Nothing to do, time to burn, some work part-time as gun-toting bandits.

My tears trickle as I remember the hope in their fathers' eyes.
I recall the passion as their fathers played for Hoppers or Empire.
I reflect on the swagger of those few who received the national prize
Of representing their country and showing their skill in cricket and soccer.

But today, too many are drugged, drunk or just sad and depressed.
Not all... because some still hope for help from the now so-called Big Man.
But for most, their hopes are dashed — basic needs remain unaddressed...
Still no relief... only despair for those men and boys below West Bus Station.

After thirty years of purposeful and unapologetic abandonment by Labour,
A community then sentenced to no development, no jobs, poor sanitation...
Wickedness perpetrated by the deceased 'Widdy-widdy bush' leader.
Yes, thirty plus years of struggle amidst the mud, rubble and degradation.

But in 2004- that was all over because we elected a new leader.
We hoped, we dreamed, we salivated at the prospect of a new community -
Certain that Grays Green would take the lead in building a better Antigua.
Confident that we would make up for those years of being treated so inhumanely.

But, now six years later... the hope, the dreams are just about gone.
The salivation is still there... but it is driven by a bitter, rancid frustration.
A frustrating realization of six years of opportunities lost and plans unborn.
Six years of stops and starts, with the rhetorical promises left undone.

My tears flow: for the men... my former students... the players I coached.
For their grand-children – born into a cycle of political abandonment
Now made worse since we have a leader who is apparently beyond approach...
A leader guided only by the whispers in his ears from the Market Street contingent.

My tears flow... these are my roots though I don't live here anymore,
And I go back, drive by and walk through hoping that something has changed.
But each time, I am left disappointed – with my heart very sore,
It is the same old - same old... seemingly with leaders just re-arranged.

And when you ask, "Have you tried to help?" the inner pain digs deeper
Advice, suggestions, ideas and much much more all proffered in vain.
Plus over the years, unquestioning, unequivocal support for this leader...
And now, massive hopes for Grays Green have given way to massive migraines.

My tears flow... Where do we go from here in this situation?
We are represented by the most powerful man in the country!
But he doesn't seem to be able to lead a Grays Green transformation...
Are the children doomed to suffer because they were born in this community?

Where is the man who supported the community cricket, netball and soccer?
Who stayed around late at night while those same boys back then played pan?
Where is the man who we loved, supported and voted for... over and over?
My anger has been so thick... I have had to read both the Bible and the Koran!

Where is my old friend... the once champion of workers from all over?
Where is my old friend once manager of Halcyon Steel Orchestra?
When I was a trainer of Empire... he worked hard hard as their manager...
Where is *our* old friend, the high ethical Grays Green's Civil Rights leader?

The Big Man – now too big to pay attention to the people who put him there?
The Big man – only open to the Middle Eastern types and their Antiguan progeny?
Largely ignoring the people who kept elevating him year after year after year –
In his own words, 'too busy in the national interest' to attend to his own community.

In Grays Green, more is at stake than just any politician's survivability.
At heart is the issue of almost four decades of dilapidation, deprivation and ruination.
And now he has been given what some say is another undeserved opportunity!
That Big Man better get it right this time – he could suffer a mass rejection.

My tears will continue to flow as I pass through my former neighborhood.
The people here are beaten and battered, and staggering on the ropes.
I used to think that the new leadership would change things for the good...
But now... I am as disillusioned as those who use dope to deaden their hopes.

When will things change? I don't know if they will ever.
If it can't be done in six years with the Big Man at the national helm...
What happens when he passes the baton by choice or with votes as a factor?
Will the children be condemned once again to more abandonment from *them*?

My eyes were once red as a result of thirty summers of tears...
Now, I am feeling blue as a result of the unfulfilled promise of the last six years...
Neither red eyes nor blue feelings are good for the soul that cares...
This is the pain of a teacher, a coach, a counselor – and yes, a friend who despairs.
These are the tears of a roots man... who now can only turn to prayers!

Tricky-dadian Disaster Capitalism?

November, 2010

"**WE WILL STOP** at nothing in ensuring that our brothers and sisters in the region receive the level of support required in this time of urgent need." This was reportedly the statement of one of the region's Prime Ministers in response to the recent devastation in St. Lucia.

Of course, the Prime Minister added that the "We will stop at nothing" assertion was conditional. She indicated that her country must benefit from any aid 'she' gave to St. Lucia. In other words, she was looking for a return on her gift. The gift, it seems, was an investment wrapped in gift paper.

Supposedly, not only was there to be a return on the gift... the giving 'in time of urgent need' might never occur if the conditions for the return benefit was not wrapped up with the 'gift package'.

Across the region the criticism of her statement has been quick and vociferous. While some people think that her comments were at least in bad taste, others think that, at worse, her comments were obscenely opportunistic and a crude attempt at capitalizing from the plight and misery of a country (and people) in need.

But, Caribbean and other countries in the so-called developing world should be accustomed to opportunistically crude offers of assistance from the so-called more developed countries. Rarely does any aid come from these countries without draconian, 'dracularian', and self-serving conditions attached.

However, most of these 'aid packages' come at the request of governments seeking 'developmental aid' for one public sector project or another. Examples are our own Antiguan Government's history of begging – sorry – asking for aid from America, Canada, China or European nations. Two examples are the construction of the Deep Water Harbour and the scandal-hit project at the airport – both under the V.C. Bird Administration. A more recent example would be our hat-in-hand request for aid from the Washington based so-called 'world bank' and the resulting 'head bowed and on bended knee' acceptance of their monetary handouts that came packaged with nefarious and draconian conditions

What surprises me now, however, is that there are 'brother and sister' countries in our region that see themselves in the role of the colonial minded, profit-at-any-cost giants of the North.

Don't misunderstand my position: If the country borrows money – we should repay it. If you beg for help and you accept the terms of such help – even if they are 'dracularian' – then you should fulfill your obligations and agreements.

The recent situation in St. Lucia is different. St. Lucians have suffered a major natural disaster. They need *immediate* help. They need *disaster relief* now. This is the time to give real 'aid' to relieve their current humanitarian plight.

This is not the time to negotiate re-development aid! Now is not the time for any country – rich or poor – to try to capitalize on the plight of the St. Lucian people.

There is a name for that kind of activity. It is called 'disaster capitalism'. And, it is sad... no... it is revolting that one of the larger and naturally blessed countries in this region would seemingly seek to introduce such an evil and monstrous practice within the family of Caribbean nations. It is *tricky*, opportunistic and predatory, and should be condemned by all.

Disaster capitalism? This has been defined as "the exploitation of a disaster (natural or man-made) to further the profits of national and multinational corporations." In practice, it is used by governments and corporations to bolster their own economies and profit margins by swiftly responding to societies in severe crises with the types of 'aid' which further their hegemonic profit-only driven corporations and public sector balance sheets. (For more on this topic read "The Shock Doctrine – The Rise of Disaster Capitalism" (2007) By Naomi Klein).

To watch the unfolding of classic disaster capitalistic maneuvers, pay close attention to what happens next in Haiti's economic development. Additionally, the so-called rebuilding of New Orleans presents a perfect study in the *tricky* ploys of 'profit-only' corporate interests supported and promoted by their government and politically elected surrogates.

I think that everyone should join in a solid rejection of this type of behavior within the Caribbean whether it is perpetrated by interests external to the region or by any Caribbean government on behalf of their corporate giants or political elite. Situations such as this should not be seen by any government – particularly a 'brother/sister' nation, as opportunities to prop up their own faltering economies, win votes at home or pay-back the corporate sponsors of their election campaigns.

No... *The indefensible cannot be defended.*

Halloween observations have just ended and this is a prime example of a terrible attempt at a horror filled *tricky-treat!* St. Lucia's disaster and the resultant immediate need for relief is not an opportunity for *tricky* political and corporate interests to reap sweet benefits from their *Trini-tricky-treat* 'humanitarian' aid!

$100 Christmas Barrels

December, 2010

CHANGING THE CHRISTMAS Dollar Barrel rules now is like moving the goal posts after the player has kicked the football, or moving the cricket stumps after the ball has been bowled!

Yes there are probably fiscal reasons for making the change. Yes, in the past there may have been abuses of the regulations. But, those are not concerns that just came to light. As a matter of fact, those concerns had been aired for several years. Any decision to make changes to the Christmas dollar barrel initiative should have been made many months ago.

Why not now? In order for barrels to arrive in time for Christmas, family members in the United States must ship barrels early. Depending on the city of export, some shipping companies recommend sending barrels in late October or the first week of November. For example, a barrel may take five or six weeks to get to Antigua if it is shipped from a non-port city like Washington, D.C. and longer if it is shipped from further West in the U.S.

What this means is that many people have already shipped barrels to their family members with the expectation that the regulations were the same as before. Families who expected to pay $1 now have to go through the regular custom process.

That is going to cost them additional money... in some cases it might be significant. (10% here, $10 there, plus warrant fees, plus $30 to fill out the warrants). Some people can afford it, others can't - like Aunt Mary from Old Road, or Pappy Sammy from Grays Farm who have to beg their great-grand children to clear the barrels for them. But of course the decision makers were silent on that issue. These are harsh economic times... even for governments. Harsh times = harsh realities = heartless decisions? What's up with this so-called Government in the Sunshine?

When the initiative was developed, the Government understood that it would lose money, but people would get their Christmas cheers without too much expense *and* without too much bureau-cratic processing.

Now, apparently, those goals and objectives (to be elected and re-elected) of the "Dollar Barrel Initiative" which were announced and pronounced with such fanfare by the Government in their 2004 Manifesto have been met and so the initiative is no longer required. "Recognizing that many families depend on food and clothes' bar-rels from relatives abroad for their Christmas cheer, the UPP will remove the duties, fees and consumption tax on these items during November and December, and recipients of these barrels will pay only $1 to clear each Christmas barrel." (Agenda For Change, 2004)

Based on the above, the UPP is now saying that people will have to pay much, much more for their cheers from the Christmas barrels. Ten percent (10%) Revenue Recovery Charge (What is that???) and $10 Administrative fee. No more freebies for Aunt Mary or Pappy Sammy (because we already got your vote)!

Of course it is expected that in these harsh economic times, the Government must ensure that it collects revenue that will help it to fulfill its many obligations and pay for Aunt Mary's medical care. However, it is similarly expected, that a "People First" 'Sunshine' Government would also understand that in harsh economic times, when the Government has a revenue short fall, that the people also have financial shortfalls. And this program, targeted directly to those most in need, was developed with that consideration in 2004. Today, people continue to be in need – *maybe more so than in 2004.*

What ought to have been decided and put in place months ago was first a process that would outline the criteria that would allow those who qualify to be recognized as "lower income individuals and their families who require the 'duties, tax and fees relief' from the Government" and who would qualify to get their "Christmas Cheer Dollar Barrel." If that step was taken, thousands of people who take advantage of the Dollar Barrel initiative would not qualify and would not be adversely affected by the change.

Those who qualified based on their "lower income status" would and should continue to pay the $1 while keeping the simplified process in place. The new regulations would then apply to all others.

I understand that an official of a ministry indicated that since there is no process to identify the so-called targeted low income individuals, the new regulation would apply to everyone.

So... in practice, the new endeavor is not really targeted to 'low income people'. It is really targeted to Christmas barrels... Well not Christmas barrels... December barrels.

Finally, I am not ordinarily a distrustful person. But, I am not so sure that the rationale given for making people's Christmas cheers more expensive is all there is to this story. For example, have the corporate comrades of the UPP elite complained about the Christmas dent in their profits because ordinary people can get their holiday goodies sent to them in Christmas barrels?

The only people who I hear cheering for the regulations of the "Dollar Barrel Initiative" are the UPP friends on Newgate and Market Streets!

Dancing with the Devil

SINCE THE GOVERNMENT of Antigua and Barbuda has embarked on its dance with the International Monetary fund, I have taken the time to examine some of the questions that many persons are asking. Can the IMF really help? What's the real cost of this assistance?

Can the IMF help? In my research the answers seem to run from a positive 'yes', through a hesitant 'maybe', to an infinitely and determinedly articulate 'no'!

I am a Clinical Psychologist... not an economist. My foremost concerns are always about people. So my question about the IMF is this: "What is their track record when it comes to helping people." Or, "Will their assistance trickle down to meaningfully help the people?"

I would like to clarify 'people'. I am not concerned with the rich or 'well-to-do' people, or even those who might classify themselves or be classified by economists as 'upper middle-class'. My concern is for the working class people... those who are struggling to make ends meet, those who used to have it marginally well but who are now on the brink of... or are already catching hell... financial and economic hell, and the people who live at or below the poverty line.

So I have done lots of reading, and truthfully, I am left saddened, disheartened, perplexed, dumfounded at the fact that our leaders have engaged in what my mother would categorize as a 'dance with the devil'.

Now I like metaphors and this one 'dancing with the devil' is quite apt when applied to the IMF!

My mother is quite a story teller – as my sons will testify! Many of her stories are uplifting, empowering, spiritual, and humorous. While some, are well... let me give you an example!

In one of her stories she tells of a businessman in the 1930's who she and her father knew when they lived in St. Vincent. The man's business began to falter and he was desperate for help. He tried to get help from banks and private lenders to no avail. He tried to sell his business. No one wanted to buy it. So, according to local folklore, he turned to the only 'entity' who was willing – even eager to help him: The devil!

It was rumored that he had made a deal. Money and riches today – and later – much much later... that dark banker who 'lent' him the money would come calling for his repayment!

Remarkably soon, his old business was booming. He started several new businesses, bought more property, and started to live the life of the very 'well-do-do'!

And after a while, most people forgot about the whispered origins of his new money. Many years passed.

Apparently... he too forgot about his 'deal'. Then suddenly one night he disappeared and for days could not be found anywhere until one morning his entrails were found hanging from the limb of the huge tree in the yard of his estate house! The rest of his body was found chained to another tree in the same yard!

That dark banker who had loaned him the money had come to collect on the agreement!

In our current dilemma, countries who dance with the IMF, are dancing with – well –not with dark bankers... but light skin deal makers and enforcers. But that is for another article.

Let me give you an example of a country who danced with the IMF.

Here... in order to do justice to the article... rather than quote it... I will display most of it so that you can read it for yourself.

In his article, **The IMF... the Negative Machine**, (*March 12, 2010*), Gabriel Banda writes that Zambia was an early example of effects of IMF and World Bank economic policies and programmes. He contends that in the 1970's, the World Bank had done a few helpful projects in Zambian sectors like education and housing. And in the 1980s, "Structural Adjustment" policies dealt with opening up Zambia's economy through privatisation, liberalisation, and commercialisation of finance and other economic sectors.

Banda writes that, "Key IMF conditions included removal of government subsidies and support of some basics facilities. Farm marketing, for inputs and prices, was liberalised."

"IMF and World Bank insisted on these conditions before lending or aiding Zambia and others. Later, some creditor governments also insisted that Zambia followed the IMF programme before getting assistance in loans, grants, and material support (from them)."

"Instead of improving as told by **Dr. IMF and Sister World Bank**, *Zambia's people experienced hardship. Some died as a result of the impact of those conditions. Zambia's capacity to do things in various fields declined. The quality of life of Zambia's individuals declined."*

"Life expectancy declined. Gains made, since independence, in education and health were negatively affected. Society was shaken. The glue of social cohesion was shaken and broken. Corruption began to increase and turn into a wide culture. By May 1987, because of the negative effect of the economic measures, Zambia's President Kenneth Kaunda announced a break from the IMF conditions."

"But IMF, World Bank, and allied creditor governments imposed sanctions. Without support from other governments

(who were) similarly indebted, Zambia later went back to the IMF programme! By force, many governments have followed IMF prescriptions. Many have had their people wounded and quality of life decline."

"In Zambia, mixed with other factors, the measures intensified in the 1990's led to great suffering and decline in Zambia's capacity to handle things in various sectors. It contributed to de-industrialisation and de-Africanisation of enterprises. Where before there had been local production, Zambia became a market for goods and services produced outside, especially by South Africa's businesses. And, through imposing policies, IMF and World Bank work against the choices and wishes of governments and peoples."

Now before you make the decision that Mr. Banda is a singular, disenchanted individual who doesn't have his facts straight, do your own research on the dangers that the IMF and its policies pose to developing economies.

I am doing my research. And **up to this point**, I cannot understand why – even in the face of desperation – would any government of a developing country turn to the IMF with their 'dark bankers' mentality'!

I understand the pressure... I understand that there is great need... but do our leaders see this really as the only way out? When will the devil come for his due? Look around in your own country, do you notice any attempts of your government any of the people's enterprises?

Remember Zambia: *"Life expectancy declined. Gains made, since independence, in education and health were negatively affected. Society was shaken. The glue of social cohesion was shaken and broken. Corruption began to increase and turn into a wide culture."*

Do those familiar?

Assk Backward vs. Ask Forwards

September, 2011

AS I SEE it, one of the issues which bedevils both political and business leaders in Antigua (and beyond) is that they are proffering "Assk Backwards" questions.

So what is an "Assk Backwards" question? It is a question which tries to understand the present by focusing on the past. For example, a business leader might look at his current sales and recognize that they have missed their projections. He or she will then say, "We had a plan.

We had a projection. We did not meet it. What happened? What went wrong?"

"What went wrong?" is a question that focuses on the past. When things don't go "right," most people look over their shoulders.

Now... let's be clear. It is important to know what went wrong. It is important to understand our mistakes. It is important to learn lessons from the things that didn't work. However, the problem with an "Ask Backwards" mindset is that leaders often get stuck there.

Not only do people get stuck in the past... they also begin to direct blame and look for the financial, economic, personnel, institutional, or other culprit that explains the gap between what was planned and what actually happened.

There is another very negative outcome of the "Assk Backwards" mindset... leaders (ministers, managers, supervisors...) become defensive. "Well, it is not really my fault... it is the global economy... (or the price of oil... the bank failures... the competition... the hurricanes, the earthquake...)!

An "Assk Backwards" mindset goes hand in hand with a "find a scapegoat" mindset. One of the excuses of people who are trapped in these mindsets is that "things didn't go according to plan". As a business consultant and clinical psychologist, one of the curious things that I have found is that in many cases there was no concrete plan. And if there was a plan... it was not well thought out, well known, or properly executed.

In many cases, the term "as expected" is probably better suited than the term "as planned". I think this is true across the board. It is true for governments, public institutions, corporations, and individuals who seek to be coached or receive counseling when their lives don't go "as expected".

Ask Forward Mindset
An "Ask Forward" mindset looks to the future instead of looking backwards. Here are examples of some of the questions:

What are our plans/goals for the next six months? Based on those plans, where are we now? And, based on where we are now, what are our projections going forward? Will we achieve our plans/goals? Let's say, for example, that the answer to the key question is that in six months we project that we will meet 70 percent of our goals. Then, the next question would be, "What do we have to do over the next six months to close the 30 percent gap – so that we do meet our goals? How can we strategically address the factors which seem to be causing us to miss our goals? What steps must we take now?

An "Ask Forward" mindset is the attitude of those leaders, managers, and entrepreneurs who have the winning edge and maintain success – despite the negative global economy, natural disasters, and all of the other things that seem to ail today's private and public sector institutions.

"Ask Forward" leaders don't wait until things go wrong to ask "What happened?" They plan ahead and look ahead. They aggressively and relentlessly monitor their current progress to see if they are still on the path to achieve their goals. And once they catch a whiff or nuance that their progress may be hindered... or that it has slowed... they jump in and do whatever is necessary to put them back on course.

The captain of a ship does not sleep at the wheel. S/he makes sure that there are lookouts. They monitor the weather, the waves, the winds... and the skyline. These days they monitor the radar and the weather channel. And so... they are rarely surprised by any sudden changes and shifts.

There is another critical feature... a crucial prerequisite... that describes effective ships' captains. They know which port they are headed to. They know where they are going. And every person on the ship knows it too. And everyone on the ship is on the lookout... Everyone on the ship has a constant mindset of "Asking Forward" questions.

Organizations, companies, and countries are in trouble if the people (customers, staff and stakeholders) don't know where the "ship" is headed. If they don't know the goal... and if they don't know the plan on how to achieve it... then they won't know when the "ship" is off course. And more importantly, if they don't know, they can't ask sound "Ask Forward" questions.

So, I recommend that on a personal level, you use an "Ask Forwards" mindset in your life. Do you have a personal vision of where you are headed? What are the details of your personal plan to get there? What are your personal milestones? How do you monitor your progress?

In your organization, have you been informed of the precise vision of your company? Have you been told of the detailed plan to achieve the vision? Do you know the role that you must play? Will you know when you, your team, your department and/or the organisation are off course? Do you feel empowered to share your perspective or take corrective action?

In our country... Well, I will leave you the reader to ask the appropriate questions regarding our nation. However, let's help our leaders to be "Ask Forwards" rather than "Assk Backwards".

End Political Arrogance in Antigua Now!

August 2011

WHETHER IT IS Mubarack of Egypt, Ben Ali of Tunisia or Gaddafi of Libya, the spotlight is now clearly focused on politicians and leaders everywhere – particularly those whose arrogant behaviors are now under scrutiny.

As I write this article the Japanese Prime Minister is fighting calls for his resignation. Former French President Chirac has been found guilty of corruption. Prime Minister Berlusconi of Italy is facing charges of sexual impropriety with a minor. In Germany, the Defence Minister Guttenberg resigned over charges of plagiarism. In China, the railways minister was recently sacked and is now under investigation for allegedly embezzling money. Those are just but a few global leaders who have recently fallen as a result of public outrage. And, there are plenty other arrogant leaders around the world in governments, public institutions and private sector organizations who should and will come face to face with the harsh spotlight of public scrutiny and the resultant outrage.

First what do I mean by arrogant? Haughty; giving oneself an inflated and undue degree of importance; believing that one has all the answers; not listening to advice from worthy and proven sources of wisdom; diminishing and belittling others while inflating one's own importance; flaunting ones authority and 'thumbing one's nose' at established protocols, rules or laws; believing that one is 'untouchable'; blatantly lying even in the face of truth and facts. I could go on, but I hope you get the picture. Do you know any political, corporate or organizational leader like that?

Although arrogant leaders are everywhere, my focus here is on political representatives. History is replete with arrogant politicians. And according to Dr. Marvin Folkertsma, history is also replete with politicians whose "colossal arrogance led to colossal horrors" for their administrations and/or countries.

Here in Antigua and Barbuda, there is evidence of political arrogance both historically and currently. One glaring case in point is the Stanford financial debacle where supporters on both sides of the political aisle were both whispering and shouting that our leaders should proceed cautiously. Recently, I heard a legal member of the current administration pleading ignorance of the dangers that that pirate of the Caribbean posed for our country. He pleaded that no one in these islands could have known that that finagling pirate was not legit! Well... my 96 year old mother was one of those who could and did see the danger. I and many others spoke and wrote and warned of the dangers. But our arrogant leaders – past and present – could only see the couple pieces of tarnished silver from the pirate's booty that were cast on the ground for them to pick up.

And even if they heard the cautions of hundreds of Antiguans and Barbudans, they were in no mood to listen because of one other facet of arrogant politicians.

That facet is a tendency of such politicians to identify their personal fortunes with the destiny of their country and the habit of identifying their personal fortunes with the decisions they make. Hence

Mubarak in Egypt led his country into an arrangement with Israel and its surrogate the United States such that, over the years, he (and his inner circle) reaped the personal benefits of billions of dollars. There is a claim that he has over $70 Billion dollars stashed away. This would make him richer than Bill Gates. True or not, he is a very, very, very, very rich man whose public salary was reportedly less than US$100,000 per year!!

Well, suffice it to say that we allegedly have some of those types right here in Antigua. Their fortunes: their fleet of cars, their houses, their lands, their swimming pools, their foreign investments, their foreign bank accounts – cannot be explained by their nice Antiguan salary. And before you jump to the conclusion that I am only referring to those who ran the country for 30 years, please take a look at some of those who have been in office for six years and are already millionaires – several times over... and shamelessly peacocking around the island.

The irony of it all is that these – particularly the new political millionaires – are some of the most arrogant ones. And, to be honest, they are newly arrogant.

Think back seven years when they were begging for a chance... arrogant? Far from it! They had a puppy dog demeanor, bowing and scraping and saying the right things to the people. They pleaded and they promised. And, eventually, they were rewarded with political power.

Today, they have taken that ballot-box reward and turned it into financial – bank account – award over and over. Not all – but many. And some of those who have not really reaped the benefit by raping the public trust, have still exhibited signs of arrogance. They have adopted this stance of being overly important to the degree that you can't talk to them and they are not approachable. And when you think you have their ear, it is so stuffed with pompousness that they either can't hear or they don't listen.

In a blog "the Real World", one writer in talking about some American politicians, contends that some elected officials believe that they know better than the people they represent. This is another sign of arrogance.

Here in Antigua and Barbuda, after they are elected, some politicians seem to take the people in their constituencies for granted. They make decisions that in some cases may not be in the best interest of the people. They ram home their decisions without consultations, without educating the people and without making (and winning) their case to the electorate. The common notion among some of these politicians is that "the people put us here to govern". That to them means that they have a free hand to do as they will with the people's enterprise, the people's future and the people's resources. We saw this with the last 'bunch' (projects such as those involving Dato Tan and Stanford, and a plethora of other examples). We see this now with the current 'bunch' – (IMF, State Insurance, purchasing dead beat real estate properties at ridiculously high prices, etc.). Who knows what's in the background and what's 'underground' in some these deals?

Arrogantly taking the people for granted also involves being dead beat parliamentary representatives for their constituencies. Some have totally neglected the people who put them there! Unemployment and under-employment are still high (maybe higher); crime is still high (maybe higher); school dropout is still high (maybe higher); the public debt is still high (some say it is higher)...

But the politicians who represent the people are doing well: their bank accounts are fatter (and getting fatter); their investments are great (and getting greater). There is no downturn in *their* personal economy...

To hear these arrogant politicians tell it... they are doing the best they can. I agree. The best they can for themselves... not for their constituents.

Let me be clear... In these sunny isles, dark arrogance is on both sides of the aisle.

Recently, I heard one of the leaders in the opposing 'bunch' ministering that a certain unelected member of the current administration should resign because of alleged past improprieties. Well that is nothing new... at least not to me. I have long claimed that those who jump fences and cross over aisles cannot be trusted. However, that aside, the leader who was clamoring for his former colleague, the fence jumper, to resign from the current administration, is also alleged to have issues of impropriety leveled against him. His strenuous criticism of his former colleague does not come from a place of enlightened change... it comes from a place of enshrined arrogance. "How dare you make one million dollars when I only got $100,000?"

So what are we to do?

I don't think that arrogance among the elected will ever go away. So what we, the electorate must do is rigorously and unapologetically hold their feet to the fire.

This means that we cannot accept illicit or unethical behavior from any politician. This means that we must demand and get total transparency from elected representatives. This means that those who seek public office must agree to have their private dealings made totally transparent. This means that political leaders must demonstrate that they are employed by all the people – including those who did not vote for them. This means that politicians must get the people's acquiescence on important matters such as those that impact our daily lives and the future lives of our children.

We must develop strong and stringent legal practices with institutions that have teeth so that we can investigate and hold potential political criminals accountable. We must find ways to separate the police from the politician and to separate the Magistrate from the Minister.

We, all Antiguans and Barbudans, must put every representative of the public trust under public scrutiny. And if their behaviors do not stand up to the ethical standards that we set and they agree to, then they must feel the weight of the people's outrage – particularly when they protect themselves from the rule of law!

We can no longer allow any politician – beloved or respected – to take us for granted. Those days are gone!

Minister Louis Farrakhan

March, 2012

WHEN I FIRST came to the United States in 1984, I kept hearing about 'Farrakhan'. But the people who were talking about him were White Americans and Jewish Americans who described him very negatively.

"Well," I thought to myself, "he must be saying something that got their attention, so I needed to hear him myself. If they didn't like him, then maybe he was saying some of the things that I was thinking, but not saying and didn't have the courage to say in public."

So over the years. I began to listen to Minister Farrakhan at every opportunity. He had a program that was on TV every Sunday morning, and guess what: I was glued to my TV every Sunday morning!

And, no, I did not agree with everything that he said. But I agreed with the direction of his discourse and I resonated with his passionate promotion of his ideas, many of which featured the continued presence of racism against people of African origin in America.

I was on the Washington Mall for the Million Man March and I have never experienced anything like that since! That day is forever etched in my memory!

His is a voice that needs to be listened to. His ideas and his themes need to be discussed and considered. After all, people listen to the Pat Robertson's of the world – people who just by THEIR rhetoric have indicated that they do not unhesitatingly and unconditionally embrace people of African origin or of any other origin except those Caucasians and Jews.

For me, I humbly say that Minister Farrakhan has kept the torch and has continued to Fan the Flames so that people like myself hear another side of HIStory – Thereby focusing on Our Story rather than Their Story....

I wasn't in Antigua yesterday... but my heart and spirit was... and thanks to my 97 year old mother... I got a full recount of his speech. By the way... my mother is a HUGE fan of Minister Farrakhan... because she says that he speaks the truth. Over the years, whenever she came to Washington, her must watch program was Minister Farrakhan on Sunday mornings. She has also watched many of his DVD's and listened to recordings of his many speeches. She is impressed with his courage to speak his truth.

Now, you may argue with me... but how can you argue with a 97 year old?

Section 2
Empowering Perspectives

My Willow Tree

January 2003

ANTIGUA IS ONE of those islands in the Caribbean that is located right in the heart of region's hurricane alley. And every year we get our fair share of high winds and rain. And some years we get more than our fair share... as a matter of fact from 1989 to 1999 we got slammed by five major hurricanes.

These hurricanes devastated the country... taking off the tops of coconut trees... lifting roofs off of some of the strongest houses, shattering smaller dwellings, destroying crops, and stripping the leaves of trees... These strong storms destroyed almost everything in their paths... except... everything except...

Except my willow tree...My willow tree...

I was born two weeks before a major hurricane slammed into Antigua. My grandfather and my mom and I barely survived that storm. We were wrested out of danger of drowning in the water that flooded out tiny house by two very caring and courageous neighborhood men. As a matter of fact, that story is featured in the very first chapter of my book Ask, Seek, Knock.

Fifty yards from where that tiny house is located stood a very old willow tree.

After that hurricane, we returned to our small one room house which had to be cleaned of mud, windows replaced and the roof repaired. I grew up there for many years afterward. And, I remember playing almost daily around and in the vicinity of that willow tree.

Now that willow tree was already old when I was a child. Very, very old. It's trunk was wide and thick and scarred. Its branches were long and tall and worn. Its roots seemed to spread like the tentacles of an octopus, stretching in every direction all around it. The old people in the neighborhood said that the roots not only spread wide... they dug deep.

It was a landmark for Antiguans everywhere. Everyone used it as a point of reference. "If you want to get to Skem's shop... you go down by the market, walk past the bus station and then you turn left by the willow tree." And if you are going to Clem's shop, "when you get to the willow – go straight down Perry's Bay..."

Every year the hurricanes came and came... house roofs got blown off, buildings were destroyed, coconut trees got their tops cut off... But that willow tree... was still standing after each of those storms.

Now I have done some research... and apparently a lot has been said about willow trees. Sir Walter Scott, the noted novelist and poet, wrote that "The willow which bends in the tempest... often escapes better than the oak which resists it!"

I can tell you that that is a spot on description of my willow tree! *Bending in the tempest...* I guess tempest is the Scottish word for hurricane.

Imagine what we can learn from that willow tree... I guess Bruce Lee – the Martial Arts Legend said it best. He said "Notice that the stiffest tree is most easily cracked, while the willow survives by bending."

The point both he and Sir Walter Scott were making was that we have got to bend even in the most furious storm... we ought not to resist when times are tough... we need to bend with the wind... go with the flow... be flexible... When the winds of change blow into our lives... we need to learn to bend like the willow or be broken like those long inflexible top heavy coconut trees.

Are you flexible or are you stiff and hard to bend? Are you top heavy with too much stuff in your brain that leads to arrogance and prevents you from bending? Do you resist change or do you easily go with the flow and bend like the bough of the willow?

Remember that other feature of the willow tree... its roots spread wide... and dug deep. How deep are your roots? Are you solid and deep in your knowledge of your job? Have you build a wide network of relationships with deep friendships? Are you rooted in your community or at work? Do you have the strong support of family, friends, neighbors, co-workers?

I suggest that you begin to embrace the characteristics of my willow tree.

A lot has changed in Antigua since my childhood days... and a lot has changed in my old neighborhood. There are now roads where there were only dirt paths. There is a conference center, a supermarket and a bank directly across from where I used to play under that willow tree. There have been many, many, many storms and floods since then.

And the old tiny house where my family and I escaped from that hurricane in 1950... it is still there today! Maybe it was built from the limbs of that willow tree...

And that willow tree is also still there – standing, bent with age, but still bending with the breeze.

And today... I am trying to be like that willow...

View Change as Challenge!

ARE YOU EXPERIENCING troubling or difficult changes on your job, at home, in your social life or in your community?

Do you see these changes as tragedies, trials or tribulations? Or do you see them as calamities, catastrophes, or unnecessary complications?

What is your response to these changes in your life or circumstances? Are you reacting in anger, fear or hostility? Or are you only irritated, frustrated, or mildly upset? Are you stressed out and threatened by the changes which you are anticipating or those which have already occurred?

In one of my keynotes on how to successfully deal with change: Change Your Life & Keep The Changes You Desire – I present over fifty strategies. One critically important strategy is that we must: View Change as Challenge!

Here are a few steps on how to do reframe "Change" into "Challenge"

First, remember this too shall pass. Think clearly about what this means. I regularly tell myself that "It is night now. Yes, it is dark. Yet, morning will come. Light will come." That does not mean that I only wait for the morning. Yes, I will bring my own light to the issue. And, I know – that eventually – things will change. For the better!

Ask yourself... What can I change in myself? What can I do, now, that will allow for me to have a different reaction to this change or these events? What about me can I change or adjust so that I can empower myself to respond resourcefully?

Rephrase the "the problem" into a "challenge" and then into a positive opportunity.

> *"There is in the worst of fortunes the best of chances for a happy change."*
>
> *Euripides.*

> *"Some men see things as they are and say 'why?' I dream things that never were, and say, 'Why not?'"*
>
> *Robert Kennedy*

Convert fear, anger and other limiting emotions such as worry, anxiety, despondency, denial or avoidance into positive energy. Energy means action. Action means doing something positive that will help to alleviate your stress and empower you to act purposefully – moving you toward a well-defined goal or outcome.

Analyze the situation. What is the problem? Look at solutions.... What can you do now? What can you do later? Who can you turn to for assistance? Who has had a similar situation like this? What can you learn from them?

Act calmly and persistently. What ever you do – take decisive and relentless action! Do not stop until you have successfully handled the situation.

Don't stop! Do not stop *after* you have successfully dealt with the challenge! Now you must take action to fortify yourself to prevent this particular issue from becoming a "problem" or from rearing its head again! This may mean: keeping your resume updated;

starting your job search today; establishing a home-based, part time business; building new and more supportive relationships; getting rid of the toxic relationships in your life; starting an exercise program, changing your nutritional habits, and supplementing your diet with vitamins and minerals; Examining your "Globe of Life" and developing a personal vision and mission for specific areas of your life.

Whenever you are faced with "change" you must view it as a "challenge" – and then as an opportunity to do something different that will lead to you having more options, more positive choices... and more personal power..

To Enjoy the Fruit –
Water Your Roots!

February 2003

"Most people are willing to change, not because they see the light, but because they feel the heat."

IT IS INTERESTING to note that every rose bush, every oak, every blade of grass, every flower's petal – is loaded with succulent liquid juices. These juices are manufactured from water that is drawn up from the soil through the roots into all areas of each plant. With the water come minerals from the soil that help to nurture and thereby mature the plant. The persistent and continuous action of drawing water and minerals from the soil results in the continuous growth and evolution of branches, leaves, flowers and fruits. This action is both continuous and persistent. It has to be. Without water and nutrients, the plant cannot be nourished and will not develop and grow.

As humans, we also need to water our roots... through study, asking questions, thinking, planning, and doing. And, like plants, we need to do these continuously and persistently. The 'sweat of our brows' implies action not only from manual labor of the limbs, but from the labor that goes on behind the brow – Asking, Thinking, Planning.

"By the sweat of thy brow..."

Isn't it interesting that personal, perspiration, persistence and per-severance all have the same root (pers...)? A key perspective of per-sistence is that it implies slow but resolute, inexorable and relentless and continuous action.

If you are determined, diligent and persistent, and if you per-severe, you will achieve your desires. H. Jackson Brown says that, "In the confrontation between the stream and the rock, the stream always wins. Not through strength but through perseverance." Visit the white cliffs of Dover in England, or Colorado's Grand Canyon or Devils Bridge in Antigua, and you will see the same law in action. The slow and relentless inexorable action of water and wind will erode the toughest rock – even if it takes thousands years.

"Genius is 1% inspiration and 99% perspiration."

Thomas Edison.

It is important to have a firm belief in the fact that your actions are moving you towards your goals. You must believe it. When we plant a seed, we do so on faith and on our experience – or the experience of others. We then water the root of the budding plant on faith... and experience. We water the root so that later we can enjoy the fruit. As a matter of fact we water the soil knowing, hoping and praying that it will make a difference at the root. And we keep watering the soil – persistently. And each day, we awake to new growth. And we keep watering.

Stop watering the soil – and the plant will wither.

No matter how long it takes, we persevere and adhere to our plan of action: water the root and we **will** enjoy the fruit – eventually - definitely.

Plant the seeds of questions, nurture the plants of answers with actions and then enjoy the fruits of your harvests.

Perseverance is not a quick fix. *It's a **sure** fix.*

A Bond of Trust

ACCORDING TO CHARLES Hazlewood, "As a conductor, there has to be, between me and the orchestra, an unshakable bond of trust, born out of mutual respect, through which we can spin a musical narrative we all believe in."

"An unshakable bond of trust" is a powerfully stated pre-requisite for any good relationship. In a world where the tenets of democracy have taken hold in the consciousness of most people, communities are demanding more from their democratically elected leaders. At the core of this demand is the principle of trust.

Communities and the people therein are saying: "You have asked for our trust. We have voted for you – and we have given you the trust that you requested." Or, "We are giving you a chance to be true to the trust that you asked for and subsequently pledge to fulfill."

Notice what people are saying: "We have made the first move of giving you our trust." Leaders are then asked to respond ethically and with strong commitment to the trust which has been bestowed on them.

However, what we are seeing around the world in large and small, developed, emerging and poor communities is that many of the leaders on whom trust has been bestowed are not fulfilling their part of the agreement. In other words there is no 'bond of trust'.

What seems to happen, in many communities, is that want-to-be leaders make the seemingly obligatory promises, then receive the gift of trust from their constituents, and in short order do everything to obliterate any opportunities for the trust that they have been entrusted with to blossom *as a result of their own efforts.*

Hazlewood's great relationship with his orchestra is one that people in many communities can only hope for from their political leaders – a hope that, in the present realities, may seemingly only be realized somewhere in the distant future.

Now, to be fair, we have seen examples in some communities, where new leaders begin their leadership tenures by appearing to embrace their responsibilities to solidify the 'bond' from their end. We have seen examples (admittedly very few and very far in between) where new leaders start their journeys by demonstrating respect for their constituents who have bestowed on them the trust. These few embark on paths where they seem to demonstrate love and commitment to the ideals that they seem to share with the people who have bestowed an open book of trust on them.

But somewhere along the journey, many of these leaders seem to develop habits of disrespecting those who have given them the gift of trust. They seem to develop tendencies not to 'spin narratives that the people can believe in' but spin narratives that they concoct – and which only they embrace and appear to believe. They spin narratives which eventually turn most of their constituents against them.

Let me be clear about the term 'spin narratives'. Narratives can be spun by the stories one tells. But narratives can also be spun by the actions one takes (or fails to take).

Thus, when we look at the narratives that some of our leaders spin (either the stories they tell or, in most cases, the actions they do or do not take), we can see that many have departed from narratives that are the same as those expected by the people they have pledged to serve. We can see that many have taken actions which shatter the bonds of trust expected by their constituents. And in their actions, they often demonstrate arrogance, disdain and an absence of respect for the people.

I want to be also clear that I am not only referencing leaders of the public sector. There are leaders in the private sector who betray the trust of their constituents: shareholders, staff and customers. Leaders, who by their actions, demonstrate an arrogant disregard and disrespect for their stakeholders and whose publicly stated beliefs and values are subsumed under privately held desires for obscene power and profit.

But whether in the private or public there may be some hope.

I attended a youth leadership forum and listened to some of the youth as they spoke about leadership, about the future and about changes to the status quo. These young people could see clearly that much of the current examples of leadership practices were not 'sustainable' and indicated that there was a deep need for a change – not only in the leaders we select – but in how we identify and train people who want to lead.

They wanted more powerful roles for the constituents who select and elect leaders so that we can 'change them quickly when they violate our trust' and not have to wait for four or five years while these people continue 'neglect' their real responsibilities. And, they wanted private sector leaders to be answerable not only to their shareholders – but to their staff and customers!

The youth wanted to develop mechanisms whereby leaders at all levels (in both private and public sectors) would be continuously evaluated to make sure that in Hazlewood's words an "unshakeable bond of trust" was maintained and that there would also be fail proof mechanisms and early warning signals to detect any 'threats' to the bond.

Finally, the youths wanted to make sure that the hopes, dreams and values of the constituency form the core of a 'belief system' exemplified by everyone and showcased by their leaders. In other words, they wanted to ensure that the narratives which were spun...

were narratives that were shared by everyone, were factual and proven, and which everyone could and did believe in.

Yes... there is hope... How far away is it? I am not sure because as I look out at the current crop of leaders (political and social) across our communities, I see the 'same old same old'. And, no – I am not referring to anyone's age! I am referring to the 'same old' type of leaders who even if they are younger, their philosophies, and most importantly, their behaviors reflect those whom they want to replace.

We need a rebirth in leaders – no matter what their age.

In Hazlewood's words, we need leaders who demonstrate and facilitate an "unshakeable bond of trust" with their constituents. We need leaders who demonstrate mutual respect for their community. We need leaders who share the same beliefs, values and principles as that of the people who uplift them and who then depend on them. We need leaders who exemplify the best interests of all of their constituents. We need leaders who are a force for good everywhere. We need leaders who are visionary and who can deliver the future that they and their constituents envision. We need leaders who practice what they preach, who are ethical and abide by society's laws and highest social practices. We need leaders who can both manage and deliver!

We need leaders who can make the world – our world – our children's world – a place where they are safer, with more freedom and where justice prevails for all.

We need leaders with whom we have not only an unshakeable bond of trust... but who fulfill and forge an unbreakable bond of trust.

Growing Seeds

November 2005

WHAT KINDS OF seeds are you sowing in the fields of your mind? 'The kingdom of heaven is like a grain of mustard seed which a man took and sowed in his field; it is the smallest of all seeds, but when it has grown it is the greatest of shrubs and becomes a tree, so that the birds of the air come and make nests in its branches.' (Matthew, 13:31-32).

All of us sow seeds. You can sow seeds of thorny shrubs, poisonous plants, or trees that bear life-sustaining fruits. Some of our most important seeds are sown in the fields of our mind. When you ask questions they become like seeds. They will blossom and bear fruit. Depending on your questions, the fruits can be bitter or sweet. I believe that many of our problems occur when we sow the wrong seeds and ask the wrong questions of life. For example, we too often ask 'why' questions when we ought be asking 'how' questions. "How can I get out of this financial mess?" Rather than, "Why me?" Or, "Why now?"

Plant seeds which will grow ideas, strategies, possibilities, and solutions to empower your life. According to Dottie Walters, "Anyone can cut an apple open and count the number of seeds. But, who can look at a single seed and count the trees and apples?" We cannot imagine that this small object - the seed - is even alive. Yet when it is placed in the soil, a transformation process is started – one that gradually – in time, will nurture and give sustenance to humans, birds and insects.

The smallest question is also like a seed. When it is put in the fertile soil of your mind it contributes to your "tree" of knowledge – which will then produce many "fruits". Yet when we look at the question (like the seed), we cannot see it's mighty potential – a potential which lies hidden from casual observation.

Like seeds, your questions will blossom larger than life in the fields of your mind and in the acres of your life.

Caution: Are you sowing seeds of thorn trees, poisonous plants or parasitic vines! Ensure that you are sowing seeds of empowerment, creative, positive possibilities and success.

By asking the right questions in the right ways, you will be transformed beyond anything currently visible or even imaginable.

Bibliotherapy: The Reading Cure

AS A CLINICAL Psychologist, I am always looking for effective ways in which my clients can help themselves at the lowest possible cost. Why low cost? Because the cost of psychotherapy can be prohibitively expensive... particularly for those who need it most. In the United States, the cost of psychotherapy sessions can range from $150 to $450 and more per session. In many cases, if the individual has health insurance, as much as 80% of this may be covered. However, many people have to make a choice between a $60 co-payment two or three times per month and buying food and paying other bills! As a result, because they have to decide on paying their rent and eating food, their mental and emotional health needs suffer.

Those clients who can afford it may meet with a mental health clinician at least a couple of times per month. Between sessions clients ought to be busy working on helping themselves heal by practicing the strategies and techniques learned from the clinician and facilitating changes in their behavioral, cognitive and emotive processes. The reason for this is that research has shown that most successful mental health outcomes are generated when people are focused on doing the assignments that help them most.

One very useful method of self-help for emotional pain such as anxiety, grief and depression is reading books.

Reading books? Yes... absolutely! It is called reading therapy!

The idea that reading can make us emotionally and physically stronger goes back to Plato. He wrote that poets gave us the arts "not for mindless pleasure" but "as an *aid* to bringing our soul-circuit, when it has got out of tune, into order and harmony with itself". The Greeks had it right! Additionally, I don't think that it was a coincidence that the Greek God Apollo was the god of both poetry and healing! The real focus of every psychotherapeutic approach is to bring the self: – behaviors, thoughts and emotions – back into 'order and harmony.'

One of those arts to which Plato referred is the art of the written word – poetry and prose. The general public benefits by being stimulated by the artists' creative use of language! Homer, Rumi, Shakespeare, Frederick Douglass, Agatha Christie, Khalil Gibran, Maya Angelou, J.K. Rowling, or the Caribbean's own V.S. Naipaul, Derek Walcott, or Saint John Perse have provided billions of people who read their works with entertainment, joy, inner peace and emotional healing when they needed it most. This is therapy by reading!

These days "reading therapy" is officially called *bibliotherapy*!

Bibliotherapy is defined as an expressive therapy that uses an individual's relationship to the written word as therapeutic relief. In some studies, bibliotherapy has been shown to be effective in the treatment of depression and the results have been shown to be long lasting. Bibliotherapy is also an old concept in library science. The ancient Greeks put great faith in the power of literature by posting a sign above some of their library doors describing the library as a "healing place for the soul".

The idea of bibliotherapy or reading therapy seems to have grown naturally from the human inclination to identify with others through their expressions in literature and art. For instance, a grieving child who reads (or is read to) a story about another child who has lost a parent will naturally feel less alone in the world. Bibliotherapy is often used very effectively with young children particularly by parents.

Among adults, reading groups (book clubs) seem to serve many purposes. They serve as social gatherings for like-minded people to discuss issues, ideas and topics relevant to their collective interests. Reading groups however also help to bring people together so that they feel less isolated and so that they can build their self-esteem. Reading groups also seem to be an experiment in individual and collective healing.

In one study, there was an indication that involvement in reading groups helped some members deal with depression, loneliness and grief. Some book clubs specifically help members who are going through the loss of a spouse, while others help their members deal with those experiencing the pain of separation and divorce. Additionally, reading specific books for therapeutic purposes is also a feature of many self-help groups such as Alcoholics Anonymous.

Thus, books seem to help everyone... whether as individuals or in groups. No matter how ill you are, there is a world inside books which you can enter and explore, and where, in the privacy of your own space, you can focus on something other than your own problems. Through reading you can give yourself a respite from the world of difficult challenges, stress, illness, chaos and disharmony.

Of course reading also serves other purposes which may not seem at first to be obviously therapeutic. The knowledge that you get from books might help you to address a nagging problem that you have. The author's words can give you much needed insight into how to manage various areas of your life. Or you may just be motivated and inspired by reading powerful stories and words of encouragement.

The benefits of bibliotherapy or reading therapy as a 'reading cure' are threefold: Identification, Catharsis and Insight. Simply stated, when reading the appropriate book, an individual has the opportunity to:

- Connect to the main idea, situation or personality;
- Engage so strongly with the story that the reader develops a deeper understanding of his or her own problems and situation;

- Develop the awareness that his/her challenge can be solved and that he/she is not the only person with this problem;
- Process, examine and walk through various paths to success;
- Develop a optimistic mindset based on the great results from the lives of the personalities in the story; and,
- Add healing dimensions and hopeful and positive patterns to inner dialogue and self-talk.

As a result of reading certain books, people are uplifted, positively influenced, motivated and inspired to heal themselves from the inside out.

The key to making all of this work is making sure you have a great book with positive stories. With so many out there, how do you know which one to choose? There are many sources of good books on the internet, at bookstores, and in libraries.

If you need suggestions specifically for emotional issues, consider visiting my website www.HealYourHurt.com.

I strongly recommend that you take up a book tonight and start reading. Relax. Immerse yourself between the pages. Journey along with the writer. Be inspired. Be motivated. Be captivated. Get ready for tomorrow – rejuvenated and reinvigorated.

And if you are hurting on the inside... and depending on your level of hurt, you may need help from a counseling psychologist.

Whether for renewal or for healing - you must make a commitment to meet regularly with your low cost – highly effective therapist – your beautiful, inspirational, informative, relaxing and therapeutic book!

Build Your Self-Esteem

PEOPLE HAVE LOW self-esteem for a variety of reasons. Some individuals suffer from poor body image and focus on all the negative traits of their physical appearance. Others have emotional issues that have caused their self-esteem to drop or feel themselves unworthy of any praise.

For whatever the reasons your self-esteem may falter, one key to building it up again is to find the root of the problem. Think of self-esteem like a house, if you build a stunning house on a poor foundation, the entire structure will eventually crumble. However, if you take steps to ensure the foundation is strong, your self-esteem may be more secure

Many individuals look for help for their low self-esteem in books or seminars. The number of available options on the market is phenomenal, and you are sure to find one on a topic that deals with your specific challenges. Check out your local library or online or offline book stores and explore their "self help" section for a book that you may find helpful. However, it is quite unlikely you will find the answers to all your problems in a book. At the very least, you may find it helpful to know others are in your same boat and that you are certainly not alone.

Additionally, you may wish to seek professional help in your quest to boost your levels of self-esteem. Often, speaking with a qualified individual can help you determine the root of your problem and the necessary path you should take for the rebuilding process. Perhaps your problem dates back to childhood, or maybe it has recently developed. Whatever the case, a professional will be able to best determine your next step.

A main factor that derails self-esteem is negativity. Negative thoughts can chip away at your confidence and crumble your self-esteem. If you find yourself surrounded by negative people or in a negative situation, try to remedy the problem. Sometimes individuals in an emotionally abusive relationship have their self-esteem shattered when a loved one constantly berates them and questions their worth.

Similarly, a negative workplace environment can contribute to the lowering of your self-esteem when colleagues or bosses excessively make very negative remarks about you and your work. Maybe you have a friend who you trust who is consistently negative and critical. Whatever the source, distancing yourself from the negativity will help you regain your higher level of self-esteem.

Strive to surround yourself with positive people. If you are going through a rough time in your personal life, you may wish to join a support group. These groups will allow you to meet other individuals like yourself and provide a forum for you to strengthen your confidence and your belief in yourself.

However you choose to begin re-building your self-esteem, start now! Since this might be a slower process than you would like, you must be persistent and consistent. Be patient, believe in the process, work steadily and stay positive. Remember, you are an important and worthy person and you should treat yourself as such.

www.HealYourHurt.com

Family Therapy as Prevention

MANY OF THE social problems which face us today emerge from challenges rooted in families. Yet, very few of the societies' responses are directed towards families. In fact, most of those responses are punitive rather than corrective. I suggest that the strategies we must use should be preventive and should be targeted to families as Therapeutic Family Prevention.

In this regard, WebMd Health News reports that when kids or teens face conduct disorders, substance abuse or other problems, family therapy may help. In family therapy, one or both parents attend therapy with the troubled child. Other family members including siblings may not have to attend even though their attendance is highly recommended because what ails one family member probably affects all of them to varying degrees.

Researcher Allan Josephson, MD says there is "abundant evidence" that family therapy can often make a big difference in six areas: conduct disorders, substance abuse, depression, anxiety, eating disorders, and attention problems.

Conduct disorders are serious violations of age-appropriate behaviors that often involve physical aggression, property destruction, and truancy, says Josephson. He continues that "There's no question that in this spectrum of family influence, conduct disorders clearly need family intervention and it's one of the more successful things when it's consistently applied,"

"It's very difficult to set limits without a child feeling secure," says Josephson. "Most clinicians that work very intensively with these problems will have a situation where a parent says, "Fix the kid,". The kid says, 'Well, why should I come in on time? Why should I stop using drugs? He or she has never done a damn thing for me.'" Josephson notes that he has had this quoted to him directly.

When the parent signs on for family therapy, that is a strong signal to the child, he notes. "The parent demonstrates their commitment to the child and the kid finally thinks, 'Maybe I should go along with this,'" says Josephson.

According to Josephson and others, engaging parents in the treatment process and reducing the toxicity of the negative family environment can contribute to better treatment engagement, retention, compliance, effectiveness, and maintenance of goals.

Therapeutic Family Prevention
Therapeutic Family Prevention helps kids quit using drugs, stay in drug treatment, and avoid related problems like truancy, says Josephson, citing "at least 12-14 well-designed studies."

Parents who strongly show disapproval of illegal drug use also helps. He notes. "This is what these public information announcements in the last few years of parents as the 'antidrug' are about."

I would go much further than Josephson. Parents who show a strong disapproval of _any_ drug use are those that send a strong 'antidrug' message to children. If a parent is sitting on the couch every night drinking a six pack of beer and watching TV – what kind of message is that sending? And can that parent then turn around and demand that their kids don't drink? Parents must portray drug and alcohol use as dangerous for everyone and particularly life threatening for children.

Therapeutic Family Prevention involves both parents and the individual child. However, there is evidence that the more family members involved in the process, the better the outcome for both the family and individual members. Thus, parents should be committed and demonstrate that commitment by full involvement in the therapeutic intervention.

The Therapeutic Family Prevention also has an intervention aspect which is directed to children who are already demonstrating interest in anti-social activities or who have started to exhibit negative behaviors. Therapeutic Family Prevention in this context does not only have a therapeutic goal, but an educative one as well. Therapists educate both parents and children about the impact of drug and alcohol use and how to deal with the individual, family and social climates and conditions which may lead to drug and alcohol use.

If you or your family is interested in Therapeutic Family Prevention find an experienced clinician who is oriented towards prevention, intervention and treatment.

Ethics In Business

THIRTY YEARS AGO, the notion that the business practices of a company should be guided by some code of conduct that protected the public, customers, staff and its shareholders alike was foreign. Indeed, the standard argument promoted by businesspeople used to be that a business's responsibility was first and foremost to its shareholders. Noted economists Milton Friedman and Alfred Carr were chief among those propagating that once-prevailing wisdom.

In a 1970 New York Times Magazine *article, Friedman wrote his now well-known argument that "a business's social responsibility is to its stockholders; therefore, the main objective is to increase profits." In 1967, Carr had argued that business is a game in which there are certain rules. He held that "a person would set aside personal ethics and values in order to meet the needs of the corporation." In other words, "corporate officials should leave their personal sense of what is right and wrong at the door when they enter their corporate offices."*

My guess is that the leaders at Enron, Merck and Global Crossing were cultured in that kind of thinking which allowed them to "set aside personal ethics and values" in order to make themselves filthy rich. As it turns out, they were not even thinking about their stockholders!

John Morse, in the *Journal of Applied Philosophy*, thinks that "Friedman and Carr are wrong, for they try to separate the moral ramifications of actions within a business environment from their effects on the individuals with whom business comes into contact. Business has to be seen as a moral entity that is an integral part of the community, and it must therefore be concerned about the welfare of the community within which it is situated, as well as the welfare of the individuals whom it influences."

Morse is right. Individuals cannot be expected to separate their personal sense of ethics and virtue from what they do on behalf of the corporation. As a clinical psychologist, I can attest to the fact, that when any individual attempts to split his or her personality in such a way, they are courting not only psychological dysfunction, but social and spiritual psychopathology! If you violate any of your personal, social or spiritual values at Corporation X during the day, you will be haunted in your dreams in the darkness of your personal soul. I've heard people say, "I wear one hat at work and another hat at home." I like to reply, "Yes, but you wear them both on the same head."

More than 25 centuries ago, the philosopher Anacharsis described the business practices of his time by saying, "The market is a place set apart where men may deceive one another." Friedman and Carr would agree... probably the former Enron executives and others would support that also. The ancient philosopher Diogenes once carried around a lighted lamp in the middle of the day and, when asked what he was doing, said, "Looking for an honest man." Of course we know what happened when Jesus went into the Temple and saw the "Money Changers" who, today, I guess we would call them financiers, bankers, traders, stock brokers, investment professionals and other corporate types. Imagine that: Corruption and thievery in the Temple of all places! I guess Friedman and Carr would have been right there spurring them on in the background... not to mention the guys at Global Crossing and Merck.

Johnson & Johnson is often heralded as a company whose ethical behavior is exemplary. Looking at how this company's core beliefs affect the way it handles critical ethical decisions may help demonstrate how a clear commitment to ethical behavior in business can define how a business operates, both inside and outside its walls.

The company apparently prioritizes its responsibilities in its corporate credo: First to its customers, second to its employees, third to its management, fourth to the communities in which it operates, and fifth to its stockholders. "Business must make a sound profit", reads the credo in describing this fifth responsibility, but at Johnson & Johnson that concern apparently comes after the rest.

In 1982 the company decided to recall 31 million bottles of Tylenol from store shelves after eight people died from cyanide-laced capsules. That recall cost Johnson & Johnson $240 million and cut its profit on $5 billion in revenues that year by almost 50%. The tampering was not the company's fault, but it decided to act even before it had complete information on what had happened. The product containers were redesigned, and new tamper-proof packaging was introduced. Johnson & Johnson's immediate response saved the Tylenol brand and won the company rave reviews. Ironically, the move turned out to be a huge marketing coup that resulted in significant goodwill from customers.

The results of such decisions rarely have the magnitude of a Tylenol case, but they are ethical decisions nonetheless. Based on what you know of the acceptable behavior of the group you belong to, you're trying to decide on the right thing to do.

In business, the pressures to remain true to one's core values are magnified, because business owners and managers are faced with competing demands to keep a company going. Does the need to make a profit outweigh the need to reward our employees fairly? Do we cut corners on manufacturing processes to keep costs down when our shortcuts may result in unsafe or polluting outcomes? Does our commitment to an employee who is in trouble outweigh the financial burden he places on the company?

Real Life, Everyday Dilemmas

A story told by the CEO of a $14 million computer consulting company points out how grueling and complex such decisions can be. A high-level employee failed to show up at a client's location one morning for a soft-ware installation. The employee was an alcoholic who apparently had had a relapse. In the end it cost his company half of its $200,000 fee from the client.

The CEO received conflicting recommendations about whether to fire the employee. Some suggested giving the employee another chance and enrolling him in a rehabilitation program. Others said the only way the employee would get help would be if he were allowed to hit rock bottom. After much agonizing, the CEO decided to offer the rehabilita-tion program.

Everything seemed fine for about eight months after the employee finished the program. Then he failed to show up for work again. This time he cost the company about $5,000. Again, the CEO had to decide what to do. The advice he received skewed toward letting the employee go, but, after some agonizing, the CEO decided to help him again.

While the CEO may have been prolonging the alcoholic's resistance to getting sober, his decision brings to life how good people in busi-ness try to do good by the people in their world, in this case a troubled employee. "Business is easy compared to life," the CEO said when retell-ing the story. "We're just laymen with good hearts and crossed fingers."

Invariably people who run or manage businesses find themselves fac-ing decisions that will clearly affect their employees' lives. Navigating through these relentless dilemmas is a day-to-day, moment-to-moment process.

Fear of Litigation

When we talk about ethical behavior in business, too frequently we're really talking about the kind of behavior people need to engage in so that they can avoid litigation. We put behavior policies in place so that we don't get sued for sexual harassment, penalizing minority workers, or slandering poor-performing employees.

With workplace litigation exploding over the past several years, the actions of businesspeople too often are driven by what will keep a cap on legal costs rather than by what we really believe is morally right.

When this happens, we relegate many ethical decisions to the human resources or legal departments and stop thinking about it for ourselves.

Fear of litigation makes even the most self-enlightened manager question his or her own judgment about employees, how to manage them, and how to be fair in the workplace. The solution is to go back to making decisions based on pre-set standards of performance, productivity and eligibility along with the documented and proven merit of a candidate rather than the fear of what may happen should this candidate not work out or not like the way we manage.

The Deeper Challenge

The deeper challenge is not merely to get businesses or corporations to change towards more ethical practices, but to get the people who are making decisions within these organizations to change the way they think -- to realize that the same care they take to behave ethically in their personal lives should drive the decisions they make in their professional lives. Therein may lie a part of the dilemma: Are leaders and decision-makers 'behaving' ethically in their personal/private lives?

One of the good things about the blurring lines between our personal and professional lives is that it makes who we are and how we behave seem more connected to our beliefs and the way we interact with other people and the community at large -- whether we're at work or not. The whole concept of "business ethics" is brought more sharply into focus when we recognize that such a notion is inextricably tied to the individuals who make up that business.

Sources:

Principal Sources: "The Good, the Bad, and Your Business: Choosing Right When Ethical Dilemmas Pull You Apart" Jeffrey L. Seglin.

    Secondary Sources: Fast Company; Caribbean Focus; Time Magazine

The Walking Wounded

WE ARE A wounded people. In this largely uncaring world, people are hurt from exploitation and victimization. People everywhere are experiencing all kinds of rape and trauma: racial, financial, political, organizational and sexual. Children are abused. Marriages are broken. Tragedies of all kinds – natural and man-made – afflict all of us. And many of these 'wounds' cut deep and last beyond a lifetime.

In many cases, these wounded people are victims of the criminal, hurtful, or selfish actions of others. In other cases the emotionally wounded have self-inflicted wounds and are victims of their own hardheaded, addictive or narcissistic actions. The outcome is the same regardless of the source. People are emotionally wounded! And so they struggle with crippling emotions such as anxiety, anger, fear, desperation, shame and guilt, hatred, depression, and low self-esteem.

The pain of such emotions is often present with us even though the incidents and relationships that caused the hurt may be long past. We have difficulty with our relationships – even those within our own households. On the job, we can't get along with colleagues. We fight with our neighbors – whether they are next door, around the corner, in the next county – or in the next country. Politically – there are fights everywhere: neighbor against neighbor; family against family; village against village, country against country.

These are the **walking emotionally wounded** who suffer as a result of 'knives' in their backs and 'forks' in their hearts perpetrated on them mostly by people who they trust, respect and depend on.

Our emotional wounds show in the insanity of our public and private actions. What else can explain a father raping his daughter or a mother killing her kids? What else can explain a priest sexually abusing young children? What else can explain a politician raping his country of the financial resources earmarked for those who need it most in his country? What else can explain caregivers who exploit the elderly and the disabled? Those people – the perpetrators of those disgusting and horrible actions – are often themselves among the emotionally wounded.

Caution! Think carefully before you decide that because you are not in this dastardly group and you therefore are not emotionally wounded!

Not everyone who is emotionally wounded abuse or hurt others to the degree that those described above do. Most people who are emotionally wounded do not abuse children and are not involved in any kind of rape – financial, political or sexual. Most appear to live 'normal' lives. Their emotional wounds and hurt are hidden deep on the inside... and only shows itself to the trained analyst and the expert eye. But those emotional wounds do wreak havoc with their lives and the lives of those closest to them.

What are some of the symptoms?

- Addiction to approval and people pleasing
- Alcohol and drug abuse
- Gambling
- Manipulation of others
- Lust for control and power

- Possessiveness
- Extreme selfishness, disloyalty and self-centeredness
- Lashing out at and hurting others without any visible signs of regret
- Eating disorders
- Kleptomania
- Shopping addiction
- High levels of anxiety
- Fear of intimacy
- Emotional numbness
- Overly sensitive
- Intensely secretive
- Very little patience or tolerance for others
- Shame and guilt
- Nightmares
- Rage and hatred – including self-hatred – and anger towards themselves
- Depression
- Sense of hopelessness leading to suicidal thoughts and gestures.
- Phobias
- Obsessive compulsive disorders
- Irrational expectations (stated and unstated) of others
- Abusive behavior including child abuse
- It shows up in their children who exhibit emotional pain by being abusive and violent; children who use drugs and become involved in anti-social and delinquent activities.

As you can see emotional wounds are a fact of life and is exhibited all around us.

There is hope, however, for those who think that they are alone in their suffering. Despite emotional and psychological wounds – there are things that they can do individually and collectively to heal the emotional wounds and improve their overall emotional health. People with emotional wounds need a lot of things.

Here are a few of the many tasks:

- They must acknowledge that they need help. This may be difficult for those who believe that their situation is hopeless. It could also be difficult for those who are intensely secretive.
- They need intensive and clinically sophisticated help through counseling and psychotherapy with expert clinicians.
- They need to feel a sense of hope. This will start them on their journey towards healing.
- They must express themselves, to talk and be listened to. In this endeavor, they need to hear themselves from the inside and at the deepest levels of their psyche. Talk-therapy could be enhanced with expressive therapy whereby the individual is allowed to express themselves in myriads of ways with the guidance of an experienced professional. In this regard, any therapeutic intervention would have to take into account the dynamic, sensitive, tenuous and potentially dangerous nature of the therapeutic process for people suffering from deep emotional trauma.
- They must accept that time does not heal emotional wounds or scars! Then they need to give themselves permission to let go of the past and heal from the inside out.
- If codependency is a factor, they need to begin recovery and healing and develop awareness in the many ways that this is a feature in their lives.
- They must uncover and then deal with the shadow parts of themselves which remain hidden from their conscious minds.

There are many resources that can help people who are suffering from emotional wounds. I encourage people to begin by reading books on emotional healing and finding clinically competent therapists and counselors to help them.

Doing Business in this Era of Globalization & Liberalization *(Part 1)*

February 2007

Radical, Revolutionary Change!

ALL OF A sudden, people worldwide are beginning to realize that we live on a small planet. Of course we always knew that earth was smaller than some of our planetary neighbors like Jupiter and Saturn. But the size of planet Earth, though comparatively small, has always presented us with giant problems whether we wanted to move around, communicate or share products and services.

Two factors impeded our progress: Distance and therefore time. Maybe the economists among us might say it differently: time and therefore money.

My mother tells me that when she was a young girl, an immigrant would travel for more than two weeks to get from Barbados to London. Of course, in those days, the only way to get there was by boat. Today, that same trip takes eight hours – by air.

Of course we don't have to travel if all we want is to see and chat with our family, friends or business partners. We can connect online! Every facet of our human experience has been transformed by modern innovations in technology. Rather than telephone calls, we now have video calls – and we don't even have to pay for them – of course much to the chagrin of Cable & Wireless and AT&T! We now use Vonage and MSN or Yahoo Messenger over the internet!

Technology has radicalized and revolutionized the way we communicate – around the world. Not only do you have a cell phone but your teenager has one also. And that cell phone (not yours... your teenagers') can hold 500 songs, maybe several full length movies, and the names and telephone numbers of 500 of their best friends (from around the world). It can connect to the internet, send and receive email, communicate through instant messages, and of course – send and receive innumerable text messages – from anywhere to any-where! And who knows? Your cell phone's capacity could be multi-plied by the power of 10 in ten years!

The world has shrunk! At least distance is no longer a critical factor and therefore, time is not the obstructive and complicating factor that it once was. And with regards to money... well many companies – particularly in developing countries and small island nations like Antigua and Barbuda – are beginning to challenge their European and American counterparts by themselves becoming multinational.

The Impact and the Possibilities of Our Shrinking World
Now, if you live in Pukanu, a village deep in the Amazon rain forest you would be excused for thinking that you live in a small world. If you sell hand crafted artifacts in the Saharan town of Timbuktu, you would be excused if you believed that you lived in a world where there was only desert and sand. That is, of course, if neither village could watch CNN International on their satellite television or go online to check their emails.

Today in 2007, the people in the village of Pukanu do have a new and expanded vision of their village and of their world. They have started the Pykany Trading Company to create a sustainable business for their community. And now they have also taken their business online. Additionally, they have a long-term contract with the Body

Shop to export Brazil Nut oil which is produced in a tiny factory for use in a worldwide line of hair and skin products. *So take note of that oil that you are using to moisturize your skin... some of its ingredients might have originated in Pukanu.*

The villagers of Pukanu understand that the world **has** shrunk and will continue shrinking. They have embraced this and have decided to take economic advantage of it.

What Is Globalization?
There are many 'definitions' of globalization. Some people see globalization as a force for economic development, prosperity and democratic freedom. Others see it as the Americanization of the world and the influence of the United States' world economically driven political hegemonic agenda. And there are those who see it as the integration of political, economic and cultural systems across the globe. For the purposes of the discussion in this paper, I will use a construct of the last definition.

Globalization is a process that has always existed. It is considered by many to be the "convergence of markets, economies and ways of life across the world." It is also thought by some to be the worldwide process of integrating and homogenizing prices, products, rates of interest and profits. Globalization relies on several forces for development: human migration, human innovation, technological progress, international trade, and rapid movements of capital and the integration of financial markets.

Within the context of globalization, *liberalization* (used in the context of economics) is the process of relaxing government rules and regulations which are considered as hindrances to international trade and the flow of capital, goods and services.

In Antigua and Barbuda we have noticed the ongoing and at times passionate debate on the pros and cons of globalization and liberalization. I will short circuit the discussion on those pros and cons to say that those movements cannot be stopped. The cat, so to speak, is out of the bag. We are all part of the global economy where we manufacture, develop, grow, trade, invest, use, share and consume money, goods and services.

A World Without Borders

Not only is the world shrinking but national borders have become more porous and many are moving towards being removed. This is a growing reality in Europe and it is fast becoming so in the Caribbean.

Although the United States of America is the chief proponent of a liberalized and globalized economy, it is the arch enemy of a borderless U.S.A. Yet, to the extent that it successfully promotes a globalized economy, is to the same extent that it is fast losing its fight against the immigrants pouring over, under and through its borders. In Antigua and Barbuda, we can see this reality in the increased human diversity in our schools, work and business places, and places of entertainment.

Globalization – whether of people or of goods and services is an unstoppable iceberg.

Can Caribbean Companies Take Advantage?

According to José Vargas Niello, in his keynote address at the 5th Caribbean Consumer Conference, "Those who support the process (of globalization) contend that there are gains such as job creation and increasing wealth for people in many countries. But there are many others who doubt that there is much gain for developing countries such as those in the Caribbean."

Without doubt, however, the Caribbean is, and has been, a market which is targeted by multi-national corporations: Royal Bank of Canada, Barclay's Bank, American Airlines, Texaco, KFC, PricewaterhouseCoopers, KPMG and many others to purchase their goods and services.

Not to be outdone, a growing number of Caribbean businesses now exist in the global marketplace and others are attempting to move quickly forward. According to Charles Nesson of Harvard Law School, "Caribbean enterprises must keep up with their international competitors and customers while ensuring that their strategy is oriented to focus on powerful global positioning."

Our Caribbean business visionaries are no longer waiting to fight the global companies on Caribbean turf. They are no longer on the defense... they have mounted a strong offense. They are taking the battle for economic success to the fertile 'developed' countries. Companies like Sagicor, Goddard Enterprises, Grace, Massy, Guardian and First Caribbean Bank are expanding in markets far beyond the borders of the Caribbean Sea.

What Does It Take To Compete (and Win) Globally?

Reflect Seriousness:
Caribbean companies make it clear that they intend to compete abroad as vigorously as the Digicel's, Royal Bank of Canada and others have competed in our territories. The leaders of these companies understand that every facet of their organizations must reflect their seriousness to contend in the world arena. Therefore, every aspect of their operations – from marketing to human resource development, from vision to mission, from sales to services, from performance to productivity – must embody that reality.

Corporate Identity
In this era of globalization, it is increasingly important for these companies to clearly establish a distinct corporate identity. Not only is globalization blurring the lines between countries, it is blurring the lines between corporations that exist in any one country or region. Therefore, these corporations must distinguish themselves by presenting a formidable and clearly identifiable corporate footprint and identity first on our turf and then abroad.

If a customer in Germany wants to do business with a bank in the Caribbean, he would need a clear distinction between banks in Barbados, St. Lucia or Antigua. How would he clearly distinguish one company from another? Where would he get this distinction? Would it be difficult to get it? Would he get it quickly or would he have to write by email and wait for a response by snail mail? Do corporate websites standout against both local and foreign competitors?

Clear *but* Flexible Identity

Dr. Kenichi Ohmae, managing director of McKinsey and Company in Japan wrote in his book, **The Borderless World**, that attaining and "maintaining a corporate identity in a global environment is different, in contrast to a centralized organizational structure." He is referring to the fact that a corporate entity that exists only in Antigua would have a different structure than would a corporate entity that existed in Antigua, Turks and Caicos, Brazil, Haiti and Miami! Caribbean companies should take note because according Ohmae, "training programs, career path planning, job rotation, company-wide accounting, evaluation systems", and human resource mechanisms and procedures that "are equitable across national borders," and that have matched "electronic processing systems" **become more important as globalization proceeds.**

In other words, as the company goes global, the visionary Caribbean company must develop the flexibility to fit itself to the differing socio-cultural, legal and market realities of the new territories into which it is venturing.

Build World Class Safeguards & Protective Mechanisms

In the aftermath of Enron and WorldCom, it is imperative that any local or regional company that has its eyes on the global marketplace, must put in place strong risk management protective frameworks to 'teflonize' it from the kinds of problems that often overtake ambitious companies and their corporate boards and managerial leaders.

Just as it must develop world class services and programs, it must equally develop first class transparency and accountability structures, practices, procedures and systems. It must develop highly visible and company-wide ethical principles and practice them unequivocally. Following these conscientious guidelines will prepare it to weather and escape the potential of turbulent threats that may lurk in the shadows of the future.

Clear and Consistent Identity
Rory Starks, a former executive officer of Food for the Hungry and World Vision, contends that the single most important factor in successfully competing globally is that an organization maintains a consistent corporate identity. How is that done? He proposes that the critical component is to have a crystal clear vision that is shared by everyone in the organization. Furthermore, as Dr. Ohmae contends, not only must there be a clear vision, but "all employees in all countries and regions that the corporation serves must unquestionably accept a system of core values that the organization has adopted."

For the ambitious Caribbean corporation, this means that there must be a continuous effort to ensure that their vision is not only clearly articulated but that there is total in-put and buy-in by its staff. In other words... their staff must opt-in to the vision – or opt out of the organization.

Starks believes that this is a monumental challenge for managers and leaders. But nevertheless, he states that having a shared vision and shared values "is one of the keys to taking advantage of the power and potential of the borderless world." Why? Because the corporate identity is tied very closely to the corporate brand... and branding is key to attaining and then maintaining an identity that will be recognized and valued within and across borders and in the real borderless sphere – cyberspace.

The issue of developing, establishing and articulating shared values is oftentimes overlooked. Caribbean corporations must clearly broadcast their value sets of customer satisfaction, maximizing staff potential, transparency, accountability, adding value to the community and leading innovation and entrepreneurship. These values will follow a company as it slowly grows into a powerful multinational entity. Indeed, its values will be a part of its distinguishing corporate identity.

Dig Deep Local Roots

Big, well known corporate identities and brands are developed in communities. In order to stand strong and stave off the strong winds of regional and global competition, a company must build a strong brand in its own backyard. It must dig deep, and develop strong local roots. It must be able to survive and thrive there first. This becomes the training ground for managers and staff. This is where the corporation learns from its most loyal customers. This is where it tests its processes, procedures and practices.

Microsoft made sure that it built a strong presence in Redmond, Washington in the U.S. At the present time, its main 'campus' is in a 300 acre corporate park with around 40 buildings and 14000 offices. The company employs over 60,000 people worldwide. But 30,000 of them are from the area around its headquarters and other areas in the region.

Of course it did not start that way – nor did it start in Washington. But, when Bill Gates expanded the company, he made sure that not only was Microsoft rooted in the Puget Sound community of Washington, it was also rooted in its own culture of technological innovation, of big ideas, of moving quickly and of being a ruthless competitor. And now, Microsoft has a big corporate identity – undoubtedly one of the biggest in the world.

Many Caribbean corporations have established strong roots in their home communities. Many add value to their community,

practice good corporate social responsibility and have been recognized for such. The problem though, is that while many have deep
roots in their 'home' communities, they have not focused on building
similar attachments to other communities in the region where they
have a corporate presence. For example, while Grace products are
widely used in Antigua, I have never heard of Grace's involvement in
any social or community activities here.

Foreign competitors don't make that mistake. Digicel, for example, has a presence in every community – almost every household – in
the region. They seem to grab every opportunity to sponsor activities
for children, the elderly, community groups, and sporting and other
entertainment events. Digicel is so deeply involved in each community, that it would seem as if it was homegrown.

If our Caribbean conglomerates are to compete beyond our borders, they must first build fortresses at home which are protected by
our communities – our people.

Entrench and Entwine
As stated above, in order for a company to build strong and stay
strong in this era of global competition, it must entwine and
entrench itself into the community. It must become a household
name. Its local staff must entwine themselves into their communities and they must be seen to be a part of the corporate entity and
local communities.

If you have been around Antigua long enough, you would have
seen investors come, start up a company and as soon as a stiff
wind blows, these 'fly by night' investors move on. They leave the
shells (buildings) of their former presence standing forlornly...
with many of them rotting until the next short term investor
shows up to patch them up... Then pretty soon they also move on
again. Many of these investors direct their activities from a far-
away home base... maybe in New York, Moscow or from elsewhere
around the world.

Our local corporate conglomerates on the other hand must dig deep and build strong. Why? Because this is their home base. From this strong, protected and supported headquarters, it can build out-stations, reach out and not only exploit, but create regional and global opportunities.

Build Locally, Think Globally
Although a local company exists in the local space, threats to its existence will come not only from local competitors but from regional and global contenders. This is already the case where companies from Trinidad, Barbados, Jamaica and much further afield are establishing themselves in Antigua and Barbuda. Antiguan companies need to maintain their focus on building teflon strong locally while thinking globally.

Everyone Should Know & Buy Into the Vision
Based on Starks' ideas, it is important to clearly define a company's key strategic initiatives or thrusts. *"Everyone, everywhere in the organization should be clear about the far reaching and multiyear directions that have been developed – the vision."*

The staff must keep their glances turned to the future as they work to make today's the company a success. They must continuously ask questions: How will things change? And how will we respond to those changes? Can we influence which things change first? What are the trends in each of our market sectors and what do we need to do to prepare for them? Who will come from over the horizon to threaten us?

Having asked those questions, staff at all levels, but managers in particular, must aggressively seek and develop innovative solutions. Then, they must take massive, continuous and unrelenting actions which are focused on a local, regional and global future. They should also develop responsive strategies and more importantly develop early warning signals and key capacities to respond quickly when threats show up.

Focus on People

In looking to the future, the local companies need to continue to focus on its staff. One major and very common error that many organizations in developed countries make is that they spend much of their focus (and resources) on technology and very little on people.

In developing countries, we make two major errors. We are slow to focus on acquiring and utilizing emerging technology and we don't focus on developing the capacity of our human resources. So local companies cannot afford to make any of those errors and not 'maximizing its staff potential' will stymie any effort to compete globally.

When we look at the Antiguan and Barbudan community, we can't help but notice that the youth have embraced the technology of the future. Adults, parents, public officials and corporate decision makers, for the most part... are dragged kicking and resisting into the age of technology. They are the last ones to have that Motorola Razr, the iPod, and yes, even the Blackberry and whatever is next. They are often the last ones to even know about the new technology – although they are the ones who can afford it. The youth lead them in both the sourcing and the use of new technology.

Now, the truth is that many other communities around the world suffer from this technophobia. But for companies that are beginning to compete in the global marketplace, such sluggishness and often intransigence by senior management can mean the loss of market space and momentum. As a matter of fact, the space that is lost will not only be in the global marketplace but will be in the regional and local markets also. Internationally, youthful entrepreneurs who live in the future are building it out today and leaving slow monolithic once market leaders in the dust much like how Microsoft eclipsed companies like Smith Corona – and much like how Google, YouTube, MySpace and Yahoo are nipping at the heels of Microsoft, IBM, HP and others.

Caribbean companies must aggressively weed out archaic thinking and embrace tomorrow's innovation – today. They must encourage their staff to embrace the cutting edge technology that increases effectiveness, efficiency and speed. And, their executive staff must show the way by themselves becoming ardent and creative users of new and emerging business technology.

The Company as an Idea Factory

Starks and others believe that companies must become idea factories in order to survive in the global tug of war. Companies must actively stimulate everyone in the organization to brainstorm radically and develop divergent new processes, products and services.

Caribbean companies have a steep hill to climb in this endeavor since most of the larger and more entrenched organizations are headed by patriarch-minded individuals some of whom still have one foot in the colonial era. These leaders believe that an individual has to "pay 'his' dues" even before 'he' can be heard.... and as a result there is a distinct bias that embraces 'experience'.

To the extent that this is evident at any Caribbean corporation, it must change along with the smashing of any gender based 'glass ceiling' that might exist. All of its junior and youthful staff must be encouraged, stimulated, influenced and persuaded to be actively involved in the process of strategically and tactically developing the company. And they must be amply rewarded not for effort... but for results.

The Caribbean corporation who desires to expand beyond its borders must also attract the best and brightest from within and without of our national borders. The fact that it may exist on a small island nation, means that the pool of world-class executives is miniscule.. if available at all. **This means that it must do two things: Aggressively develop home grown talent while attracting proven experts from the global marketplace.**

Indeed, the latter is a key feature and benefit of globalization and liberalization for any local company with global aspirations.

Doing Business in this Era of Globalization & Liberalization *(Part 2)*

March 2007

Focus on the Three Engines of Globalization

LEADERS OF ASPIRATIONAL Caribbean companies must focus on the three key engines that drive globalization. The first of those three engines is *technology.* According to Micklethwait and Woolridge, authors of "A Future Perfect – The Challenge and Hidden Promise of Globalization", technology is a 'messy marvel' that is chaotic and unpredictable in its spread throughout the world. They write that "Technology gives entrepreneurs ... the freedom to challenge giant companies and to break up concentrations of power." They also contend that technology gives people the power to weave connections all over the world. It frees people from the boredom and 'tyranny of place.' It has certainly done that for the Pukana villagers in the Amazon rainforest and it can do so for the various business entities in the Caribbean.

Because of technology consumers can surf the internet and look for the best deals on products which are available anywhere in the world. Because of global telecommunications networks, workers in India, for example, are processing insurance forms, running Swissair's back office, talking to General Electric's American credit card users, even monitoring security pictures sent by satellite to 'guard' office buildings in California. Last week, I talked with a customer service representative who works for Vonage, the American Broadband telephone company. He told me he was in the Philippines. I had called a U.S. toll free number.

There is a small company in Antigua whose business activities entail them to speak several times each day with product suppliers in Chicago and Boston. A year ago, their Cable and Wireless telephone bill was five figures. This year they are making more calls and paying less; A lot less: US$49.95 per month. And that involves a fax line. If a supplier leaves a message, the staff can retrieve it by phone, by email or on the internet – capabilities that C&W's ancient technology didn't and couldn't offer.

The ability to use tomorrow's technology today is key. Companies who exist in small island nations like Antigua and Barbuda can get a jump on the traditional international corporation by skillfully developing and manipulating the technological inventions as soon as they are released... and even before they are perfected.

Speed & Service
There are two other key advantages that using new and emerging technology will bring to Caribbean corporations: Speed and Service! One thing separates today's successful companies (large and small) from yesterday's monoliths: the ability to move quickly. Goods and services are quickly moved around the world by technology masters like FedEx and UPS. Money is quickly changing from being paper and coin to becoming molecules moving either through a wire or being transferred wirelessly (or a combination of both) virtually going from one end of the earth to another sometimes in nanoseconds!

Comprehensive information about each of a company's customers should be captured in a database. This would allow the business to keep in contact with them (particularly for those who have email) advising them of new services and products and updating them on critical issues that would normally concern a customer.

Even more importantly, whereas the average Antiguan customer may not have been exposed to some of the emerging technologies, consumers in distant locales may already have such exposure. What this means is that the aspirational corporation must embrace and use advanced technologies which may not be locally mainstream but are already mainstreamed in their target markets.

Like customers of American and some European banks and companies that offer other services, Caribbean customers expect and should get expedited and integrated services. We need to be able to go online and not only see our bank balances, not only transfer money from one account to the other, but we need to be able to look at the checks from our checking accounts that have been processed and to see who signed them and when. When we sign in we need to be able to see not only our bank accounts, but we should see our insurance and investment accounts. Caribbean banks, for example, need to use the technology to integrate all of their services thereby allowing for the deepening of customer relationships through cross-selling and by tailoring services and products on the spot to the specific needs of individual customers. To compete effectively abroad, local companies should offer world class services at home.

Last month, I visited a branch of an indigenous bank to do some transactions. The supervisor saw me looking at a brochure on his desk which was promoting some of the banks offerings and asked if I was interested. That was good. But he should have been able to access my account and know which of the various services of the Bank I was using. He should know which of the services I had been offered... by whom and when! And he should have known if there was any product or service for which he could have offered an upgrade. Today's technology allows a company to fully integrate and federate information on customers from all sectors of its business.

Flexible Technology Architectures

All across the world, companies are rushing to create new products and services that bring additional value to individual customers. For example, banks are moving quickly to optimize back office processing and core banking systems with one aim: faster and improved quality services to customers at lower costs. This innovative flurry of activity leaves little time for hesitation. Caribbean executives don't have the time to form a committee, discuss the matter for six months, take it to the Board and wait for a decision. They need to be empowered to make decisions now... role out new, processes, products and services, then make adjustments as they go. Technology, quality services and speed go hand in hand.

Caribbean corporations also need to continue enhancing their real-time technological architectures by blending different infrastructures across their various entities. For example, when a customer applies for a loan, a credit card or an insurance policy, basic information about the customer is automatically filled into the application form by the system... even if the customer has just moved to another Caribbean country!

Capital

Capital is the second engine that Caribbean companies must embrace. Micklethwait and Wooldridge observe that financial markets "are not just wiring economies together and altering the structures of companies, they're also changing entire political systems." I can stay on my hotel verandah at Jolly Beach Vacations in Antigua and invest in stocks, or trade on just about any stock market in the world. Billions of dollars are flying around the world electronically with just a touch of a key on a keyboard here (in Antigua) and a keyboard there (in Pukanu). Decisions to buy and sell, to manufacture and to provide services are made and transacted in cyberspace.

To maximize use of limited capital, Caribbean companies must also become adroit at building cross-national relationships and developing global partnerships. In many cases, our home grown companies do not have the necessary capital to market their products and services in markets outside the region. Thus, they must attract strategic partners and negotiate beneficial symbiotic relationships to launch sustained successful multi-market and cross-border offensives and initiatives.

Management
The third engine is management. Micklethwait and Wooldridge posit that the internationalization of business practices now has its own momentum, and that it is also accelerating. According to them concepts like reengineering and economic-value added practices are being practiced by "organizations as diverse as the British Treasury and Thai Farmers Bank PLC."

Recognizing the explosive growth of global enterprises, international consultancies and top business schools have helped to seed a global canon of management development. In December, 2006, Yale School of Management decided that its first year MBA students will study abroad during the first two weeks of the second semester as part of the school's International Experience, a mandatory component of its new curriculum.

In this context, Caribbean companies must exponentially build the capacity of their management staff to produce and perform on the world stage. Although multinational companies have always operated in small Caribbean countries like Antigua and Barbuda, they never really had any local competition. Of course, there are a few exceptions. In Antigua's case there was ACB – the famous 'penny bank'.

In today's business environment, the decision makers of your competitor sits in Houston, London, Toronto, Tokyo and in some cases – farther away. Such a decision maker could well have been a graduate of both the law and management schools at Harvard, Yale, and/or Oxford. In addition, she probably manages a budget in the hundreds of millions, and directs a work force of over 10,000 people world-wide. She has probably been an executive in three or four other mega-companies and takes home an annual salary in excess of US$3 million with bonuses that will top US$20 Million.. or more! And she… is not (yet) the CEO, President or Chairperson of her company!

She represents the leadership profile of managers with whom our Caribbean executives are competing.

Therefore, you can understand why we must develop world class managers. Caribbean companies are competing with international heavyweights with world class executives. Therefore, we have to build the management and leadership capacity to compete at the global level.

Managers must first see themselves as competitors in the global marketplace. They cannot compare themselves with the borderline competent managers in the company next door or with the seriously limited administrator in the government office up the street.

Managers must be exposed to both world class training and world class experiences. They must be knowledgeable and be able to articulately converse and skillfully negotiate with their global competitors and partners. **They must demonstrate their ability to function at the highest levels.... Not within their company... but in any company – and not within our country – but in any country!**

Managers must be qualified, certified and excel in their specific areas of expertise. **But that is not enough.** They must also develop a keen understanding of, and competencies in all areas of the business enterprise... and in many areas outside of the company's businesses. They must know where their company is going and how it's going to get there. They must be adroit at turning obstacles into props and become business transformational experts. And, they must have the spirit of entrepreneurs and the expertise of world class administrators.

Our National Trailblazers

In Antigua and Barbuda and indeed the West Indies, we have historical evidence that we can... not only compete globally, but that we can do so and win. At least we used to win – as a matter of fact – we were once the best. And we did so, with leadership from our local trailblazing heroes.

Of course, I am talking about cricket – West Indies cricket! For a significant period – some contend for over 15 years, the West Indies dominated world cricket – a multi-nation – global enterprise. And, in Antigua's case – our local heroes led by Sir Vivian Richards, Richie Richardson, Andy Roberts, Curtly Ambrose, Ridley Jacobs and others competed at the highest level of world cricket. They know what it takes to win in the arena of global competition when you are up against – not only the best cricketers in the world – but some of the world's most powerful countries who stand fully behind their cricketers.

Our companies can take a page from their book of experience, knowledge and skill: Confidence, assertiveness, unwillingness to lose, skill in your area of expertise, all around competence, commitment to the team, focus on development, and maintaining their sharp readiness to compete.

Globalization at Work and at Play

These days the West Indies Cricket teams are not doing well in the global arena. But in a few weeks they will have the chance to get back their winning edge right here at home.

It should not be lost on our local and regional companies that the Cricket World Cup will be held here in the Caribbean – bringing sixteen nations to our shores. The world is coming… invading our shores.

This is globalization at work and at play.

And right at this moment, our local and regional companies should be strategizing on how we might in turn visit the fertile shores of the invaders.

She Had Found Her Voice
Nurturing Our Children's Talents

March, 2007

I AM SITTING here at the car dealership having my car serviced. Of course, I am expecting not 'sticker shock' but 'bill shock'!

It is 8:40 a.m. and those of us here in the waiting room are being informed and entertained by the CBS Morning Show.

First there was LL Cool J who has teamed up with Subway to promote their new 'healthy meals' message. Amazingly, he gave away a bicycle to a member of the audience!

Then the host of the show introduces a young, petite girl who can't be older than twelve. Her name is Madeline Edwards of Goldsboro, North Carolina. She is a classical singer and she is about to sing us one of those... I guess 18th Century Mozart pieces...

Oh well... boring... I yawn, take my eyes off the TV and continue thumbing through and scanning the sports pages of the Washington Post.

And then she begins to sing! For the next three minutes I am mesmerized and transfixed!

First, that is not her voice... Nope! Impossible! That voice could not be coming from that tiny, petite, small figure. This is not the voice of a twelve year old. *It is not the voice of an eighteen year old!*

This is the voice of a seasoned adult classical singing superstar. Absolutely... This is the equivalent of Pavarotti, Ella Fitzgerald, Michael Jordan and Tiger Woods all rolled into this small girl.

Everything is there... tone, control of vocal variety, pitch control, presence and poise, delivery... If she is this good now... how much better can she get?

Wow... Wow!

Her proud parents were standing on the side just as mesmerized as everyone else... on the set and off the set... and out of the set!

Folks I can tell you this. That young girl is going to be busy for the next few years...practicing and perfecting her art. She will not be involved in negative, anti-social activities. She is already busy... fine tuning her voice... not that there was any evidence that it needed to be fine-tuned!

Are her parents lucky? I don't know how much effort they have had to put in to help her 'find her voice'! I don't know how much time and effort they have put in taking her back and forth to music practice. I don't know how much money they have put into paying for her lessons.

What I do know is that having found out what she loves to do and what she is good at doing and what she wants to do, they are fully committed to helping her getting better. As a parent myself, I know that I try to do everything I can to help my sons find their natural talents – to find that one or two or three things for which they may have that extra inclination or special love for.

And, that is hard to find. Although her parents are lucky... I am sure that it is not – and has not been easy for them.

For the rest of us, our children may never be the Louis Armstrong, Maya Angelou or Martina Navratilova at soccer, poetry writing or mathematics. But it is in helping them search for and find the things they love and things in which they have special interest or inclinations where the real journey to success is. Though this journey is hard... it is the journey where they are most likely to find themselves.

And most importantly, while they are on the journey to finding themselves... they are going to be busy... very busy. They will not have much time to get involved in antisocial activities. Their exposure to negative peer pressure... though still present... will be lessened by their focus on positive things and by being surrounded by positive and supportive people.

Madeline Edwards' parents have helped her to find her voice... literally.

Our job as parents is just that: Take our children on a journey of finding their talents and keeping them busy while doing that. *This is one of the secrets of successful parents and successful young adults and teenagers that I reveal in my Prevention For Parents.*

By the way... it was obvious that Madeline was extremely excited and having a lot of fun while she mesmerized her TV audience.

Let's Not Call Them Thugs!

March, 2011

AS THE RECENT incident at one of our secondary schools sug-
gests, not only are we faced with violence involving youth in the community, such violence has weaved its way into our schools.

One would hope that the school is the place that society can
expect to be violence and drug free. Sadly, that is not the case – not
in Antigua and certainly not elsewhere. There are countries around
the world where schools are fortified with metal detectors, cameras
in the hallways, guards patrolling hallways, policemen at the doors
and in patrol cars circling around the block, and a general sense of
fear by everyone – students, teachers and administrators. This worst
case, nightmare scenario has not yet arrived in Antigua.

But is it far away? If there is a threat of that, then something must
be done quickly to slow and then halt the progression towards that
frightening scenario.

However, knee jerk reactions by teachers, parents, school officials
and government leaders will only provide temporary, feel-good band
aids. Expelling students from school – be they thirteen or eighteen –
will potentially turn youths who are inclined towards violence into
hardcore violent adults. The act of expelling students is one that
also turns them loose into a society where there are no formal (or
informal) programs that could help to turn them around – plus give

them another chance at being educated. In expelling them... we are literally – not figuratively - abandoning them.

The young men involved in this recent incident could possibly be incarcerated. If this happens, they will be shoveled into a prison where they will be mentored and coached by older, seasoned and even more violent criminals. And, who knows what other experiences they will be exposed to there?

Yes, I know that there are many persons who will say that this is what they deserve. Their behaviors do need to be addressed. But how we address them and the behaviors of other youth who increasingly exhibit similar tendencies will mean the difference between influencing them to adopt socially acceptable behaviors or forcing them to degenerate into hardened, lifetime criminals.

Let's think this through.

- If we shunt them off to prison to punish them (as their behaviors seem to deserve), what effect will that have on them and on their future?
- Do you think that this experience (expulsion, and potentially prison) will 'teach them a lesson' – a lesson that will transform them into 'good young men'?
- Are there behavior modification programs in the prison that will help them to 'see the error of their ways' and teach them to adopt more socially acceptable behaviors?
- Will they be taught (in prison) the knowledge and social skills they need to contribute meaningfully to their own development and to the development of a nation that needs positive, skilled, creative, resourceful and energetic young people?
- Are there community-based programs that will help them to modify their behaviors, teach them pro-social skills and help them not only to continue their education but motivate them to be more academically successful this time around?

- Are there community-based programs that will teach them work-related skills if they are not doing well academically?

Zero Tolerance Policy

Certainly, without question, a Zero Tolerance policy in schools is the way to go: Zero drug use; Zero drug activity; Zero violence; Zero guns or other weapons; Zero threatening behaviors! Zero... Or else!

One of the things that perturbs me is the 'or else'!

I don't think that we have thought through the ramifications of the 'or else' and what it will do to these youth – who no matter their behaviors of today – represent our nation's tomorrow. Frightening... isn't it? To shunt them off to an institution where there is no proven intervention or rehabilitative program is to *'further deny'* them the possibility of contributing meaningfully and positively to our future and more importantly – to their own future.

It is because they represent our nation's tomorrow why we must go beyond our angry assertion that punishment is the answer to this troubling issue.

Yes... they must be held accountable for their actions.

But we, adults, must be held accountable for our non-actions. What do I mean?

I know that many of you have questions about the phrase above: *"Further deny them"*. What did I mean by that?

Well, this is not the first violence activity related to that school and many other schools in our nation. The issue of violence and criminal activity among our young people (in or out of school) has been in and out of the public spotlight for years.

So what have we done to address the slow, yet constantly encroaching violence, drug involvement and other criminal activities in and around our schools? Where are the intervention programs? Where are the prevention programs? Where is the training for teachers and other school officials? Where are the community programs that would empower our youth to adopt more pro-social thinking, behaviors and lifestyles? Where are the training programs for parents so that they are tooled with the skills and techniques to help them in their increasingly difficult task of parenting? Where are the programs to boost the efforts of community groups and churches and to give them the kinds of training they need to help in a synergistic and integrated island-wide effort at prevention and intervention?

Our failure to put these things in place is a failure at our level to recognize that these problems will not go away on their own. The public angst that has shown up around the current violence should be accompanied with public shame at the fact that we have not developed sustained, serious and proven attempts at helping youth who may be headed in the direction of, and the destination to which these young people seem to have arrived.

Did anyone see it coming? What were their behaviors like – prior to these incidents? Are there any records that document prior negative behaviors? How were they doing academically? What was their attendance like? What were their relationships like with teachers and other students? Did any of them have sessions with the school counselor?

As a former official with the District of Columbia Public Schools and as a former teacher at the Greenbay Government School – and as a parent, I can unequivocally say that these behaviors did not just show up on the day of the violence. It was a long time coming. The question is: Who noticed? And what could they do about it? What was in place to help these young people address their growing destructive behaviors?

Let me put on another hat. As a clinical psychologist, I can also say that there is a possibility that such behaviors are themselves cries for help. Just like in cases of suicide, subtle cries for help when they go unnoticed, can grow into full blown violence (at self or others) and other destructive behaviors.

In failing to notice cries for help – and in failing to address such cries for help... we adults fail our young people.

I want to be clear that I am not pointing at any specific individual or institution. I am not criticizing any government agency or official. I am saying that we all must hold ourselves accountable.

And, rather than seeing such violence only as a chance to punish, we should see such violence as cries for help by youth who need help... who know they need help... and who know they are not getting the help they need.

Rather than seeing the youths involved in this incident as the only ones who need help... we should look around – open our eyes and see that – potentially – there may be tens of other youths in each school (including elementary schools) – who are crying out for help.

Thugs?

Madam Minister, locking "the thugs up" will send messages to other youths. You are right about that. But are you sure that the message that you intend to send is the message that they will receive?

I strongly disagree with identifying these youths as 'thugs'. That kind of labeling of misguided youth who commit violent acts will not help them or other youths. While their behaviors might be 'thuggish', I am sure that if you meet with some of those young people one-on-one you would be left with a different perspective of them. And if you dig deeper what you find might surprise you!

I have worked as a Clinical Psychologist with youth in a juvenile detention facility housing at times over 400 young men. Many of them had committed atrocious crimes (including homicides). However, when I met with them individually, I could not but privately lament to myself that somewhere, at some time, someone had dropped the ball.

Individually, these were misguided, and yes, often violent young people who had committed serious crimes. Many of them had failed in schools. Most of them were from poverty stricken homes and neighborhoods infested with adult drug use and deadly adult violence. Most of them were already using drugs. Many of them had parents and family members who were already involved in the criminal justice system. And, some of them had been diagnosed with mental health disorders –after they were incarcerated.

But one thing stood out. All of them aspired to something better – something different. They just didn't know how to get there! My job – our job – was to have them understand that what they were doing would not get them what they wanted... and then to get them to buy-into using more pro-social methods of achieving the 'success' and different life and lifestyle that they secretly wanted.

Were their behaviors thuggish? Yes.. absolutely so! Would I call those children thugs? **No**.

Let's reserve words like 'thugs' for hardcore criminals with a long history of violence and 'mayhem'. I have also worked with 'thugs' – some of the worst criminals from the District of Columbia: Drug king-pins; serial murderers; serial rapists; serial child-sexual abusers. Thugs? Yes.

These kids in **our** schools are not thugs!

Let's not drop the ball with the young people here in Antigua who are involved in violence and other negative behaviors... whether they are your children, someone else's children or mine. They belong to us... negative behaviors and all.

In November, 2006, I wrote an article entitled **"Violence and Drug Prevention Needed"**. As a matter of fact, I thought it was so important that I included it in one of my books: **Radical Thoughts & Empowering Perspectives** (the precursor to this book). In that article I indicated what I thought needed to be done to **prevent** us from getting to where we are today.

In that article, I give a brief outline of the school and community based **prevention** programs and strategies that I suggest we implement across the nation to stem the slowly increasing tide of violence and drug use among our youth.

Today, I suggest that the authorities look for best practices and demonstrably, proven, successful programs from across the world that will help us in the effort to **foster resilient and law-abiding youth** who are focused on their educational, professional and personal development. I also encourage them to develop critically needed intervention programs to help youth like those who were recently involved in that violent incident.

About the Author

Marcus M. Mottley is a business consultant, clinical psychologist, executive coach and business owner with more than 35 years of experience in the fields of education, mental health, and human resource and organizational development. He develops and presents keynotes and seminars nationally and internationally, and provides consulting services to corporations, associations, government agencies and community organizations.

Dr. Mottley works with private and public sector organizations in the Caribbean, the United States and Europe, and has executive coaching clients worldwide. He has a strong record of having successfully completed performance, productivity and climate assessments within organizations and has helped to address cultural competency issues, resolve team conflicts, build human capital capacity, and effectively resolve human resource challenges within public and private sector organizations.

www.ingramcontent.com/pod-product-compliance
Lightning Source LLC
Chambersburg PA
CBHW062207280526
45788CB00001B/485